The Yoga Kitchen

The Yoga Kitchen

**OVER 100 VEGETARIAN RECIPES TO
ENERGISE THE BODY, BALANCE THE MIND
& MAKE FOR A HAPPIER YOU**

Photography by Lisa Cohen

quadrille

ALL THE RECIPES IN THE YOGA KITCHEN ARE:
- Vegetarian
- Gluten-free
- Refined sugar-free

VEGAN (V):
Throughout the book, the **(V)** sign indicates
that these particular recipes are suitable for vegans!

INTRODUCTION

Welcome to The Yoga Kitchen! This book isn't just for yogis who practise yoga on a regular basis, it is for anybody who wants to balance their mind and energise their body by feeding themselves health-conscious vegetarian dishes, free from gluten and refined sugar. Each chapter is designed to improve our lives with recipes that support our core and create a greater synergy between our mind, body and spirit. The Yoga Kitchen follows the yogic principle that by combining our diet with our holistic health we can unite and strengthen our entire system. This book aims to bring this yogic philosophy into your kitchen and also into your life.

Each chapter is designed to help, support and transform the different energy systems within our bodies called the chakras; Ground, Flow, Vitalise, Nurture, Strengthen, Calm and Pure. They each provide different types of nutritional support which target various parts of our bodies. When reading this book, it is important to focus and concentrate on deciphering how you feel; what your body craves and how you want to personally evolve and develop, as this will lead you to the right chapter for what you need.

The central belief to The Yoga Kitchen is that by concentrating on what we need and reacting accordingly with the food we eat, we can all correct and align our balance, energy and happiness.

The chapters in this book are based on the ancient yoga chakra system. The system came to the West from the ancient traditions of India, where they originated more than 4,000 years ago. It can be seen as a collection of homes in our bodies for our spiritual, mental, emotional and physical elements. It helps us navigate the connection between our inner- and outer-worlds, creating an alignment through a set of seven portals, which we move between throughout our lives.

The Yoga Kitchen has been inspired by my journey through yoga and the synergy I see between it and my own naturopathic experience. I believe that if our health is to be transformed, the process must begin from within. Integration of mind, body and energy makes healing possible. It is not enough to simply understand what needs to be done without action and it is not enough to move without understanding of what needs to be moved. It is the integration of these two actions that can create long-lasting health and can bring change into our lives. In the same vein, the food choices we make throughout our lives need to be in balance with our emotional needs and overall bodily functions.

By eating The Yoga Kitchen way, I hope you will all become energised, balanced and ultimately more happy!

HOW TO USE THE YOGA KITCHEN

The Yoga Kitchen has been divided into seven chakra-based chapters, which each represent yogic energy centres within our bodies. Each chakra is associated with different emotions, organs and body systems. The recipes in each chapter have been created to help you strengthen and balance that chakra, emotional need and body system.

The goal is to ascend from the root chakra in the Ground chapter to the crown chakra in the Pure chapter, through the various chakra stages. The beauty of this system is that it not only helps us to discover who we are, but it also helps us to create who we want to be. By bringing awareness to each energy centre we can discover more about ourselves and strengthen aspects, which we feel, are integral to who we are and who we want to become.

Ground

Location in the body:
The base of the spine.

State of mind:
For when you want to feel: secure, energetic, balanced, vibrant and passionate.

How you want to feel:
For when a sense of belonging and community is needed in your life. When you need to find your sanctuary, to anchor back to your roots and be reminded of your home.

Flow

Location in the body:
The sacrum located between the pubis and navel.

State of mind:
For when you want to feel: the juices of life flowing through you again, enthusiastic and confident.

How you want to feel:
For when a sense of movement, growth and change is needed in your life. When our vital force is depleted and our digestion feels sluggish.

Vitalise

Location in the body:
The diaphragm located between the navel and the heart.

State of mind:
For when you want to feel: energised, powerful, happy and hopeful.

How you want to feel:
For the moments when a sense of empowerment and will are needed in your life. These recipes will fuel you, providing you with the will and determination to choose the right path to take.

Nurture

Location in the body:
The heart.

State of mind:
For when you want to feel: nourished, loved, natural, youthful, rejuvenated and intelligent.

How you want to feel:
For the moments when a sense of gratitude and caring is needed in your life. These recipes will evoke emotions of conviviality, caring and sharing within you. These recipes should be shared with others and made with love.

Strengthen

Location in the body:
The base of the neck.

State of mind:
For when you want to feel: tranquil, calm and steady.

How you want to feel:
For when you want to be able to speak your mind and live authentically, tranquilly and calmly. For the moments when you need to find a sense of harmony between your body and mind. Cook these recipes when you feel your heart and mind are in conflict.

Calm

Location in the body:
The centre of the forehead.

State of mind:
For when you want to feel: focused, calm,
sophisticated, logical and wise.

How you want to feel:
For the moments when a sense of self-reflection
and wisdom is lacking. Make these recipes when
your imagination needs a boost and perspective is
needed in your life.

Pure

Location in the body:
The crown of the head.

State of mind:
For when you want to feel: cleansed,
light, powerful, centred and have a
deeper understanding of yourself.

How you want to feel:
For when you want to feel rejuvenated, clean
and pure. Choose these recipes when simplicity
and intent is needed in your life and you need
to feel pure.

MY YOGA STORY

Brought up in a Sicilian/British household in Australia, my Sicilian grandmother had a passion for simple healthy food that tasted great. It was from the depths of her kitchen that she taught me to create mouth-watering recipes that had remained unchanged through countless generations before her. Over the many years I spent in her company, under her watchful eye, I came to learn the art of cooking as well as adopting many of her underlying cooking principles.

Initially, the idea of turning my passion for cooking and all things related to food bypassed me as a possible career path. Fascinated by natural health, I graduated from the Southern School of Natural Therapies with a four-year degree in Naturopathy. I practised for many years, supporting the health of my patients' with challenges including weight loss, infertility, hypertension and many different types of cancer. It was during these years that I began to understand how the body is intrinsically related to its environment and what we feed it. I specialised in Nutrition & Herbal Medicine, which led me to develop a strong understanding of how our bodies heal and interact with their surroundings.

By 24, my curiosity of unexplored shores could no longer be ignored and like so many others of my antipodean generation, I ventured off to chase new sunsets. My step into the unknown took me to the rolling hills of the Chianti region of Tuscany, Italy. After eight months spent enjoying the pleasures of hot summer days, lazy afternoon siestas and the abundance of Italian produce I embarked on my next adventure to the French Alps, which was to become my home for the next two seasons as a chalet chef.

And so, with two years of summer to winter seasonal chef jobs under my apron strings, I found myself moving to London on a whim of love. Having been swept off my feet by an Englishman, I took a position as a private chef in Notting Hill and continued my journey with food in the metropolis.

My first experience of yoga didn't come until a friend of mine invited me to join her for a class one evening. After an hour of twisting, stretching and sweating my way through a dynamic power yoga class I collapsed onto my mat utterly exhausted but also feeling completely alive. Somehow I had found peace, elation and clarity in the process of moving through the combination of these ancient poses. My ongoing experiences of the yogic way of life seeded the idea to open The Retreat Cafes. I began to work in conjunction with established yoga studios which enabled me to provide healthy-eating, vegetarian cafes, provide home delivery services and market the yoga retreats I now run around the world.

NATUROPATHY

Naturopathy is a natural treatment, which recognises the existence of vital curative forces within the body. It believes that by treating the human body as a whole, one can remove the root cause of the disease rather than treating individual parts or offering symptomatic remedies. It is underpinned by a fundamental principle, vis *medicatrix naturae*, the healing power of nature made clear by Hippocrates over 25 centuries ago. Hippocrates described health as an 'expression of a harmonious balance between various components of man's nature, the environment and ways of life,' meaning nature is the physician of disease.

Naturopaths believe that we can only achieve health if we live in accordance with our environment, connected to the vibrational energies of the universe and nature around us. The physical, mental, emotional and spiritual forces within our bodies are all seen as one, creating a whole.

The key aspect to how a naturopath views the human body is the recognition of a vital force energy, seen as the same energy which flows through the universe and nature. A depletion of this vital force is believed to be the root cause of illness. A naturopath will seek to restore this vital force to a patient, so the body will heal itself naturally. Besides the vital force, health is also maintained with proper nutrition, rest, sunshine, hydration and occasional fasting.

COOKING NOTES

ACTIVATED NUTS

Activated nuts are simply those which have been soaked to enable the natural process of germination to occur increasing their nutritional value. It allows the nuts to go back to their original purpose as a seed and provide food and all the nutrients needed for growth. It's a secret trick Mother Nature uses and when you begin to harness this tool and really tap into it, the results are boundless. It is easy to soak your own or you can buy them ready-activated. You will find several recipes that call for them throughout the book.

ORGANIC

Where possible buy organic ingredients, especially for items which are difficult to wash, such as broccoli or strawberries and fruit that you will use the skin in the cooking, such as lemons and limes. And for eggs or for variable-quality ingredients, such as matcha powder.

RAW HONEY

Most honey sold today has been heated and filtered, robbing it of its nutritional value and resulting in a product no more valuable than a simple processed sweetener. Raw honey can contain up to 80 different substances important to human nutrition. Besides glucose and fructose, honey contains: all of the B-complex, A, C, D, E and K vitamins, minerals and trace elements: magnesium, sulphur, phosphorus, iron, calcium, chlorine, potassium, iodine, sodium, copper and manganese. The live enzyme content of honey is one of the highest of all foods. Honey also contains hormones, and antimicrobial and antibacterial factors and is thought to have probiotic properties, so helps to increase your good gut bacteria, thus aiding digestion. It is well worth investing in raw honey and finding a honey producer you can buy from direct. Your local farmer's market may be a good place to start. In recipes where I have used honey, you may prefer to substitute it for a vegan option, you can use either pure maple syrup or coconut nectar.

HIMALAYAN SALT

In some recipes I choose to use Himalayan salt as I find it isn't as 'salty' as sea salt. So, I use it in recipes which require just a hint of salt. Himalayan salt contains all 84 elements found in our body. Benefits include regulating the water content, promoting a healthy pH balance in our cells, particularly brain cells, blood sugar health and helps to reduce the signs of ageing.

SEA SALT

I choose Maldon sea salt flakes as I love the flavour it adds to food. However, feel free to use any sea salt. If possible, do avoid standard table salt as it is highly processed and devoid of its natural nutrients.

COLD-PRESSED COCONUT OIL

If you don't mind the sweet coconut flavour of this oil, you will be laughing all the way to the good health bank every time you to cook with it. Coconut oil is the most stable cooking oil (over 400°C/752°F) to use. Although it is considered a saturated fat, it is the richest source of medium-chain fatty acids. These medium chains (as opposed to long-chain triglyceride fats) are smaller, therefore easily digested and are immediately burned by your liver for energy; like carbohydrates, but without the insulin spike. Coconut oil actually helps to boost your metabolism and helps your body use fat for energy. If coconut oil is unavailable, use extra-virgin olive oil to cook with instead, ensuring you don't heat it above 130°C (266°F) or reuse it more than once.

EXTRA-VIRGIN OLIVE OIL

Olive oil is a monounsaturated oil, so it helps to lower cholesterol by blocking cholesterol absorption from food. It improves cardiovascular function and digestion by improving liver and gall bladder function and increases bile flow while also stimulating pancreatic enzyme production. It acts as an anti-inflammatory and antioxidant agent and stabilises essential fatty acids against oxidation. (I source mine from the same organic Tuscan olive grove where I lived for two years www.patrignone.com.)

FILTERED WATER

I recommend you use filtered water for all the recipes. This removes impurities, including a percentage of heavy metals and, in my opinion, gives it a better flavour too.

AVOCADO

I prefer the flavour of hass avocados, as they are lovely and creamy, with a distinctive, nutty taste. They are the most commonly sold in the UK. Their skin is thick and black and so can be easily eaten with a spoon to scoop out the flesh. All avocado recipes used throughout this book are designed with the hass avocadoes.

EGGS

Choose free-range organic eggs. Look for the code 0, which is a legal requirement in the UK for all farmers to stamp on their eggs as proof of growing conditions. (Please see list below for other coding.) Eggs are medium unless otherwise stated. Anyone who is pregnant or in a vulnerable health group, such as very young children or the elderly should avoid recipes using raw or lightly-cooked eggs.

UK egg codes:	
0	Organic
1	Free-Range
2	Barn
3	Cage
UK	Origin
12345	Producer ID

COOKING TEMPERATURE & TIMES

I always use a fan oven. If your electric oven is not fan-assisted, increase the Celsius temperature by 15–20°C. All cooking times are approximate and should be used as a guide only.

PREPARING FRESH PRODUCE

Always wash fresh fruit, vegetables and herbs and peel if necessary (but leave edible skin on when you can to improve your insoluble fibre intake).

SPOON MEASURES

All spoon measures are level unless otherwise stated: 1 teaspoon = 5 ml, 1 tablespoon = 15 ml.

VEGETABLE & FRUIT SIZES

These are all medium or average-sized unless otherwise stated

CUP MEASURES FOR VEGETABLES

If measuring leaves, such as baby spinach or pea shoots, always pack as many as you can into the cup without damaging them (or it will hold hardly any!).

Ground

In this chapter the recipes focus on root vegetables, earthy foods and plant-based proteins. So, the ingredients in this chapter all stem from root-based plants that are high in insoluble fibre. Our bodies must be nourished with ingredients from the earth in order to grow. These ground-based recipes are the solid foundations for lifelong health and wellbeing. The sanskrit name for the ground chakra, *muladhara*, also means root. This chakra anchors us to our bodies, our physical surroundings and to the earth, so in the same way a plant cannot survive without its roots, neither can the human psyche without its core grounding. Our roots represent where we have come from and the elements we need for physical survival and health – what we eat, drink, breathe and hear.

Disconnection from the body is a cultural epidemic. We often over- or under-eat, deprive ourselves of sleep and function on artificial stimulants to keep up with the demands of a faster society. Of all the losses rupturing the human soul today, this alienation is especially damaging because it separates us from the very roots of existence; our grounding. It has become all too easy to lose our dynamic connection with our body, but by listening and eating from within we can begin to unlock the true power of our bodies and minds.

In order for us to find true health, our body must have its foundations firmly placed in the roots of the earth in order to survive and thrive. Grounding ourselves makes us feel safe, alive, centred and at one with our environment.

Pictured L–R (text on opposite page): Almond Butter and Hazelnut Butter

ACTIVATED NUTS

To activate raw nuts, place the required amount into a bowl that will hold them comfortably and cover with filtered water. Add a pinch of sea salt and leave to soak at room temperature for 8–12 hours or overnight. These are now activated and can then be dried if required. Preheat the oven to its lowest temperature, drain off the water from the nuts, spread them out on a baking tray (baking sheet) and place in the oven until completely dry.

SPICED ALMOND BUTTER (V)

MAKES 450ML (15FL OZ/ SCANT 2 CUPS)

A staple in my kitchen, a dollop of this butter on apple slices makes for the perfect snack.

500g (1lb 2oz/3¾ cups) raw almonds, activated
½ teaspoon sea salt
½ teaspoon ground allspice
½ teaspoon ground cinnamon
2 teaspoons vanilla bean paste or vanilla extract

Preheat oven to 160°C fan/350°F/Gas 4 and roast almonds for 15–20 minutes, until they are lightly golden.

To make the butter, place the almonds and salt into a small food processor or high-speed blender and pulse until the almonds resemble coarse crumbs. Add the spices and vanilla paste and begin to blend the almond crumbs, stopping to scrape down the sides of the food processor. The almond oils will start to be released from the nuts and they will begin to turn buttery.

Blend for an extra minute or until you have reached the consistency you desire. Place the butter into a clean, screw-topped jar and store in the refrigerator for up to 1 month.

HAZELNUT BUTTER (V)

MAKES 450ML (15FL OZ/ SCANT 2 CUPS)

Nut butters are a great source of clean proteins. Just 100g (3½oz/ 1 cup) raw hazelnuts (filberts) will yield 15g protein. Feel free to add a tablespoon of raw cacao powder to this recipe to make your own chocolate hazelnut spread. My cupboard is never complete without these healthy 'bacio kisses'.

500g (1lb 2oz/3¾ cups) raw hazelnuts (filberts), activated
raw cacao powder (optional, to make chocolate hazelnut butter)

Preheat oven to 160°C fan/350°F/Gas 4 and roast hazelnuts for 15–20 minutes, until they are lightly golden.

To make the butter, place the roasted hazelnuts into a small food processor or high-speed blender and pulse until the hazelnuts resemble coarse crumbs. Begin to blend the hazelnut crumbs (and cacao powder, if using), stopping occasionally to scrape down the sides of the food processor. Although the hazelnuts will start off looking quite powdery, when the oils start to be released from the nuts, they will begin to turn buttery.

As soon as the hazelnuts turn buttery, blend for an extra minute or until you have reached the consistency you desire. Place the butter into a clean, screw-topped jar and store in the refrigerator for up to 1 month.

SWEET POTATO SCONES

MAKES 8

Root vegetables used in baking bring elements of both savoury and sweet to a recipe. Adding moisture and a binding texture, puréed root vegetables are the solution for healthy baking recipes. Start experimenting!

90g (3¼oz/scant 1 cup) ground
     almonds
2 teaspoons gluten-free baking powder
35g (1¼oz/¼ cup) buckwheat flour
pinch of sea salt
½ teaspoon ground cinnamon
½ teaspoon ground ginger
½ teaspoon ground nutmeg
1 egg
180g/6oz/¾ cup) boiled or steamed
     puréed sweet potato
2 teaspoons vanilla extract
½ teaspoon pure maple syrup
30g (1oz/¼ cup) walnuts, roughly
     chopped, plus extra to decorate

Preheat the oven to 180°C fan/400°F/ Gas 6. Line a large baking tray (baking sheet) with baking paper (parchment paper).

Whisk together the ground almonds, baking powder, buckwheat flour, sea salt and spices in a medium mixing bowl.

In a small mixing bowl, whisk the egg, sweet potato purée, vanilla extract and maple syrup, until it is a smooth paste. Add the sweet potato mix to the dry ingredients and add the chopped walnuts once incorporated.

Using an ice-cream scoop, scoop mixture onto the prepared baking tray and sprinkle extra chopped walnuts onto each scone (biscuit). Bake in the oven for 15–18 minutes until risen, golden and the bases sound hollow when tapped.

Remove from the oven and allow to cool on the baking tray. Store in an airtight container.

DUKKAH EGGS WITH BROAD BEAN & AVOCADO MASH

SERVES 2

There is no better way to start the day than with the combination of nuts and eggs. Clean plant-based proteins make this an ideal pre-yoga breakfast. Dukkah is an Egyptian spice blend traditionally made from roasted nuts, seeds and spices. It can be stored in an airtight container in a cool, dark place for up to a month.

For the dukkah
1 tablespoon coriander seeds
1 tablespoon cumin seeds
1 tablespoon fennel seeds
1 tablespoon black peppercorns
100g (3½oz/⅔ cup) raw hazelnuts (filberts), lightly roasted
100g (3½oz/⅔ cup) raw pistachios, lightly roasted
50g (2oz/⅓ cup) sesame seeds, lightly toasted
50g (2oz/⅓ cup) sunflower seeds, lightly toasted
1 teaspoon sea salt
½ teaspoon sweet paprika

For the broad bean & avocado mash
100g (3½oz) shelled fresh or frozen broad beans (fava beans), skins removed (or if unavailable use shelled fresh or frozen peas)
flesh of 1 ripe avocado
handful of coriander (cilantro) leaves, washed
finely grated zest and juice of 1 lime
sea salt and freshly cracked black pepper

For the eggs
2 eggs
2 tablespoons distilled white vinegar
2–3 radishes, thinly sliced, to garnish

For the dukkah, place the coriander, cumin and fennel seeds in a dry frying pan and toast for 2 minutes or until fragrant. Place in a mortar and pestle and pound together with the black peppercorns until finely ground.

Place the hazelnuts, pistachios, sesame seeds and sunflower seeds in a food processor and pulse until a chunky, sand-like texture forms. Add the pounded spices, sea salt and paprika and quickly pulse together. Taste and adjust the seasoning. Place the dukkah in a shallow bowl and set aside.

To make the mash, place all the ingredients in a bowl and roughly mash using a fork. Taste and adjust with more lime and sea salt if needed.

To poach the eggs, heat 4cm (1¾in) of water in a deep frying pan over a low heat until just simmering. Add the vinegar and use a wooden spoon to create a whirlpool. Crack each egg into a small mug and then slip into the water. Poach the eggs for 3–4 minutes until cooked to your liking. Remove with a slotted spoon and drain well.

Coat the poached eggs in the dukkah mix, then serve on a bed of the broad bean and avocado mash, garnished with radish slices.

BUCKWHEAT BEETROOT WRAPS

MAKES 12 CRÊPE-LIKE WRAPS

Disillusioned by the mass produced gluten-free wraps available I decided to come up with my own creation for the yoga-eating masses. The vibrant red colour of these wraps makes them both nutritionally and visually beneficial, however, carrot or spinach juice would also be a great substitute.

Buckwheat flour is superbly nutritious and is actually completely gluten-free despite what its name implies.

240ml (8¼fl oz/generous 1 cup)
    beetroot (beet) juice
2 eggs
175g (6oz/1⅓ cups) buckwheat flour
1 teaspoon ground cumin
½ teaspoon salt
2 tablespoons olive oil
90ml (3fl oz/⅓ cup) water, to thin
a little coconut oil, for frying

For the filling
hummus and filling ingredients of your choice: avocado, cucumber, roasted sweet potato wedges, rocket (arugula), mixed seeds, and a squeeze of lemon juice

Put the beetroot juice and eggs in a large mixing bowl and whisk until combined. Now add the buckwheat flour, cumin and salt and whisk together, slowly adding the water and olive oil until the mixture is smooth. Allow the mixture to stand for about 15 minutes at room temperature to thicken slightly.

To cook the wraps, heat a thin crêpe pan or frying pan over a medium-high heat and rub a little coconut oil over the pan. Pour about 60ml (2fl oz/ ¼ cup) of the batter into the pan and swirl the pan around to create a thin crêpe. Cook for 1–2 minutes until bubbles gradually pop over the surface of the crêpe and it loses its glossy look. Flip the crêpe using a spatula and cook for a further 30 seconds before removing from the pan. Repeat with the remaining batter using a little coconut oil each time. Place each cooked crêpe on top of each other (depending on your pan, the subsequent crêpes will require much less time to cook than the first one as the pan heats up).

To fill, take a cooked crêpe and spread hummus over the inside surface (the side you cooked second), then add the filling ingredients of your choice. Either roll the wrap into a tight roll or simple fold it in half and enjoy.

SWEET POTATO, GINGER, TAMARI & MAPLE SOUP (V)

SERVES 6

The warmth of the ginger and lime combined with the sweetness of the maple syrup and the sweet potato gives this soup its complex, deep flavour.

1 tablespoon melted coconut oil
2 red onions, peeled and roughly chopped
Himalayan salt and freshly cracked black pepper
8cm (3¼in) piece of fresh ginger, peeled and sliced
4 large sweet potatoes, peeled and roughly chopped
2 litres (68fl oz/8½ cups) vegetable stock
60ml (2fl oz/¼ cup) tamari soy sauce
90ml (3fl oz/⅓ cup) pure maple syrup
juice of 2 limes
2 tablespoons coconut milk, to garnish

Put the coconut oil into a large, heavy-based saucepan, add the onions, along with a pinch of salt and sweat gently over a medium heat for 5 minutes or until soft and translucent, stirring occasionally. Now add the ginger, sweet potatoes and toss to coat. Crack some black pepper and sea salt into the saucepan and cook for a further 10 minutes over a medium heat.

Pour in the vegetable stock and bring to the boil. Immediately reduce the heat to a simmer and cook gently for 25 minutes or until the sweet potato begins to fall apart when prodded with a fork. Remove from the heat and leave to stand for 5 minutes, then using a hand-held blender, purée until smooth.

Stir in the tamari, maple syrup and lime juice. It's at this stage that this soup really becomes your own. Check for seasoning, then adjust the flavouring to your taste using more salt, tamari, lime juice and maple syrup to create a deep, warm, sweet and lightly zingy soup. Spoon over a little coconut milk to serve.

TURMERIC CAULIFLOWER STEAKS & KALE (V)

SERVES 4

2 small cauliflower heads
90ml (3fl oz/⅓ cup) melted
   coconut oil
2 teaspoons ground turmeric

For the sundried tomato pesto & kale
250g (9oz/1⅔ cups) sundried tomatoes
100ml (3½fl oz/scant ½ cup) extra
   virgin olive oil
40g (1½oz/¼ cup) blanched almonds
1 large garlic clove, peeled
½ teaspoon dried oregano
½ teaspoon sea salt
½ tablespoon balsamic vinegar
500g (1lb 2oz) kale, washed, stems
   trimmed and leaves gently broken
   into small pieces

For the stuffed mushrooms
12 chestnut cup (cremini) mushrooms
2 red chicory (Belgian endive) heads,
   any damaged outer leaves removed
150g (5oz/scant 1 cup) mixed
   olives, pitted
2 garlic cloves, peeled
Himalayan salt and freshly cracked
   black pepper
4 clementine segments, to garnish

Preheat the oven to 180°C fan/400°F/
Gas 6. Remove all leaves from the
cauliflower heads. Cut two large
2cm (¾in) thick slices from the
widest part of each cauliflower head.
Place the slices on a baking tray
(baking sheet) lined with baking
paper (parchment paper) .

Place the coconut oil in a saucepan
over a low heat. Mix in the turmeric and
then baste each cauliflower steak with
the turmeric oil using a pastry brush
and making sure to cover the surfaces
completely. Bake the cauliflower steaks
in the oven for 25 minutes or until
golden, tender and cooked through.

For the pesto, place all the
ingredients, except the kale, in a food
processor and blend until smooth.

To make the stuffed mushrooms,
remove the stalk from each mushroom
and place on a chopping (cutting)
board. Place the mushroom caps on a
non-stick baking tray (baking sheet).
Remove 4 chicory leaves from each head
and set aside for garnish. Place the inner
heads of chicory on the chopping board
with the olives and garlic and, using
a large knife, chop all the ingredients
finely. Place in a bowl and mix together,
then season with salt and pepper. Using
a teaspoon, scoop the finely chopped
mixture into each mushroom cap and
cook, uncovered, in the oven for
10 minutes.

Meanwhile, make the tomato pesto
and kale. Take 4 heaped tablespoons
of the pesto and massage it into the
kale. When the oils and vinegar start to
soften the kale, it is ready.

To plate, place a dollop of the
remaining pesto on each plate, then add
the massaged kale. Place the cauliflower
steak in the middle of the plate and tuck
the reserved chicory leaves under the
cauliflower steak. Scatter the chestnut
mushrooms and the clementines around
each plate, then serve immediately.

MUSHROOM RAGU (V)

SERVES 2

If there is one vegetable (or fungi) which connects us to the earth more than any other, it's mushrooms. It must be their earthy taste and ability to take on rich flavours. This recipe can be whipped up after a long day at work in 5–10 minutes. This ragu can be served with courgetti (spiralised courgettes/zucchini), sweet potato gnocchi (page 84), over a baked sweet potato, or simply eaten alone with a slice of gluten-free sourdough bread (see page 50).

1 tablespoon coconut oil
600g (1lb 5oz) chestnut mushrooms, sliced into 1–2cm (½–¾in) pieces
4 garlic cloves, thinly sliced
2 tablespoons tomato purée (paste)
½ teaspoon raw cacao powder
½ teaspoon sweet paprika
300ml (10fl oz/1¼ cups) vegetable stock
5 sprigs of thyme
Himalayan sea salt and freshly cracked black pepper

Heat the coconut oil in a large frying pan and sauté the mushrooms and garlic over a medium–high heat until golden brown.

In a small bowl, mix together the tomato purée, raw cacao powder and sweet paprika, then add to the mushrooms. Reduce the heat to low and coat all the mushrooms with the paste.

Now add the vegetable stock and thyme. Stir together and allow the sauce to bubble and reduce for 10 minutes. Season to taste and remove the thyme sprigs and serve.

JUICE PULP BURGERS WITH PORTOBELLO MUSHROOM BUNS

MAKES 4 BURGERS

There's nothing more satisfying than a burger... especially when it uses left over ingredients. Pulp from juicing can be used for all sorts of food and beauty recipes. Try using cucumber pulp for cleansing the skin, carrot pulp for carrot cake and beetroot (beet) pulp for these delicious burger patties. Whatever your everyday life throws at you these beetroot burgers are designed to restore your depleted energy levels.

For the fennel slaw
1 fennel bulb
2 asparagus spears, very thinly sliced
1 tablespoon fresh dill (dillweed), chopped
1 tablespoon fresh parsley, chopped
juice of ½ lemon
1 tablespoon white wine vinegar
1 tablespoon olive oil

For the juice pulp burger patties
100g (3½oz/generous ½ cup) cooked white quinoa
1 tablespoon olive oil
½ small red onion, finely diced
2 garlic cloves, finely chopped
200g (7oz) beetroot (beet) pulp
1 teaspoon chia seeds
1 teaspoon fresh rosemary, finely chopped
2 tablespoons quinoa flakes
50g (2oz) goat's cheese, rind removed
1 egg, beaten
½ teaspoon sea salt
2 tablespoons hemp seeds

For the buns & topping
8 Portobello mushrooms
4 cos (romaine) lettuce leaves
1 avocado, halved, stoned (pitted), peeled and sliced
4 slices halloumi, grilled (broiled)

Trim the fennel, then cut in half. Using a mandolin, slice very thinly. Place in a bowl along with the asparagus slices and chopped dill and parsley. Add the lemon juice, white wine vinegar and olive oil and toss together. Season to taste.

Now make the patties. Preheat the oven to 180°C fan/400°F/Gas 6. Place the cooked quinoa, red onion, garlic, beetroot pulp, chia seeds, fresh rosemary, quinoa flakes, goat's cheese, egg and salt into a large mixing bowl and stir to mix all the ingredients together. Set the mixture aside for about 30–40 minutes, to allow the chia seeds to coagulate. Using wet hands, divide the mixture into 4 portions, then roll each portion into a flat round patty. Place the hemp seeds on a flat plate, then roll the edges of each patty in the seeds. Place each patty on a baking tray (baking sheet) lined with baking paper (parchment paper). Bake in the oven for 15-20 minutes.

While the patties are baking, place the Portobello mushrooms, face down, on a lightly oiled baking tray and bake for 10 minutes or until just cooked. The mushrooms should start to wrinkle on the sides and be just warmed through.

Remove the patties and mushrooms from the oven and place a mushroom, skin side down, on 4 plates, then begin to layer each with a lettuce leaf, avocado slices, beetroot patty, halloumi and shaved fennel salad. Place another Portobello mushroom on top, serve and enjoy.

CARROT GNOCCHI WITH CASHEW CREAM & GREMOLATA

(V)

SERVES 4

In the plant kingdom, there exists one seed, far superior to any other as a source of clean protein. The newly popularised hemp seed contains up to 30% highly digestible protein. This recipe provides a perfect ratio of amino acids and essential fatty acids found within the body naturally and the most abundant and easily digestible source of clean protein available in our food chain.

For the carrot gnocchi
3 carrots (350g/12oz), peeled and
    chopped into pieces for roasting
1 tablespoon olive oil
120g (4oz/generous ¾ cup) raw
    macadamia nuts or cashews,
    activated (see page 19)
1 tablespoon grated fresh ginger
1 tablespoon pure maple syrup
1 tablespoon tamarind paste
1 tablespoon ground cumin
½ teaspoon ground coriander
½ teaspoon sea salt
micro leaves, to garnish

For the gremolata
1 bunch of parsley, leaves picked
1 garlic clove, peeled
zest of 1 lemon

For the cashew cream
120g (4oz/generous ¾ cup) raw
    cashews, activated (see page 19)
2 tablespoons preserved lemons,
    chopped
60ml (2fl oz/¼ cup) rice milk
pinch of sweet paprika
pinch of sea salt

To make the carrot gnocchi, first roast the carrots. Preheat the oven to 170°C fan/375°F/Gas 5. Boil (parboil) the carrots in water for 3 minutes. Drain and toss in the oil. Spread out on a baking tray (baking sheet) and roast in the oven for about 40 minutes until tender and lightly golden. Place the roasted carrots, soaked macadamia nuts, ginger, maple syrup, tamarind paste, ground cumin, coriander and salt in a food processor and blend until smooth. Taste and adjust the seasoning.

Next, make the gremolata. Finely chop the parsley, place in a small bowl, then grate the garlic clove into the bowl using a microplane grater or a fine-toothed grater. Grate the zest of the lemon into the bowl and mix together. Set aside.

Now make the cashew cream. Combine the cashews, preserved lemons, rice milk, sweet paprika and sea salt into a high-speed blender or small food processor and blend until creamy. Adjust seasoning.

When ready to serve, place a spoonful of the cashew cream in the centre of the dish and, with the back of a tablespoon, smear it across the plate. Place the carrot gnocchi on top of each cashew cream swirl, then sprinkle the gremolata around the plates and serve.

VAMPIRE JUICE (V)

SERVES 2

Of all the root vegetables beetroot (beets) are by far the leader in terms of health and nutritional benefits. Their earthy and sweet taste is just a disguise for their liver cleansing abilities. A strong antioxidant and blood purifier, beetroot also contains glutamine, an amino acid, essential to the health and maintenance of the intestinal tract.

1 large beetroot (beet), cleaned and stems removed
2 carrots, thoroughly scrubbed but not peeled
½ cucumber, rinsed
125g (4oz/1 cup) fresh cranberries (or any other seasonal red fruit such as blood orange, watermelon or pomegranate)
2.5cm (1in) piece of fresh ginger, peeled

Simply, pass all the ingredients through a juicer and serve.

COCONUT BEET ICE-CREAM (V)

SERVES 4

This recipe harnesses the ultimate flavour combination of beetroot and coconut.

Arrowroot is pure starch often used in gluten-free cooking. It helps to thicken liquids at lower temperatures than cornflour (cornstarch), is not weakened by acidic ingredients, has a neutral taste, does not turn sauces cloudy and is not affected by freezing. Used here in home-made ice-cream the arrowroot helps prevent ice crystals from forming during the freezing process.

500ml (17fl oz/2¼ cups) coconut milk
2 tablespoons arrowroot
360ml (12fl oz/1⅔ cups) beetroot (beet) juice
50g (2oz/¼ cup) coconut sugar
2 tablespoons vanilla extract
½ teaspoon salt, or to taste
toasted coconut chips, to decorate

In a small bowl, whisk together 250ml (9fl oz/generous 1 cup) coconut milk and the arrowroot. Set aside.

In a medium saucepan, heat the remaining coconut milk over a low heat. When heated to almost boiling, add the whisked coconut milk and arrowroot mixture and keep stirring until thickened, then remove from the heat.

Now add the remaining ingredients to the saucepan and whisk until smooth. Leave to cool, then chill in the refrigerator.

Once the mixture is cold, either place it into an ice-cream maker and churn until frozen or line a large loaf tin (pan) or glass baking dish with clingfilm (plastic wrap), making sure there is enough clingfilm hanging over the edges to cover the top as well. Pour the mixture into the lined container, cover and place in the freezer. When it is semi-solid (after 2–3 hours), whisk it again with a fork or spoon to break up the ice crystals and refreeze. Make sure the ice-cream is covered each time it goes into the freezer or ice crystals will form and create an 'icy' ice-cream instead of a smooth, creamy consistency. When frozen, place in a food processor or blender and process until smooth. Cover and refreeze until ready to serve.

Serve in scoops, topped with toasted coconut chips.

CHEWY TAHINI & ALMOND COOKIES

MAKES 10

These cookies hit the post-exercise spot every time! They take no time to make and can be kept for up to a week without drying out. The moment I unlocked the versatility of tahini and its smooth texture these cookies were born. Tahini comes in both, light and dark varieties and is packed with calcium, which supports bone structure and strength.

220g (8oz/2¼ cups) ground almonds
½ teaspoon sea salt
1 teaspoon gluten-free baking powder
200g (7oz/generous ½ cup) raw honey
    or coconut nectar
200g (7oz/¾ cup) tahini paste
2 tablespoons vanilla extract
raw pistachios, roughly chopped,
    to decorate

Preheat the oven to 170°C fan/375°F/ Gas 5. Line 2 baking trays (baking sheets) with baking paper (parchment paper) or patisserie mats.

Place the ground almonds, salt and baking powder in a large mixing bowl. In a small saucepan, mix together the honey, tahini and vanilla. Place the saucepan over a medium–low heat and stir until combined and the mixture has begun to thin a little.

Pour the contents of the saucepan into the dry ingredients and stir together to form a dough. The dough should come together in your hands quite easily and feel quite warm and soft. Allow the mixture to stand for 10 minutes to cool and firm slightly.

Roll the dough into 2.5cm (1in) balls then place them at 5cm (2in) intervals on the prepared baking trays as the cookies will spread during baking.

Using a fork gently flatten the balls, then add a few roughly chopped pistachios to the centre of each.

Bake for 8–10 minutes or until lightly browned round the edges. The cookies should feel soft while warm but will harden. Wait until the cookies have completely cooled before removing from the baking trays. Store in an airtight container.

MASALA CHAI CARROT CAKE

MAKES 1 LARGE 26CM (10IN) CAKE

This is the ultimate carrot cake. It's unbelievably moist because you use ground almonds instead of flour and balanced due to the warming cinnamon, ginger and allspice running through it.

60ml (2fl oz/¼ cup) boiling filtered water
1 Masala chai tea bag
10 eggs
150ml (5fl oz/⅔ cup) extra virgin olive oil
340g (12oz/1 cup) raw honey
grated zest of 2 oranges
½ vanilla pod (bean), seeds scraped out
800g (1lb 12oz) carrots, grated or processed in food processor
200g (7oz/2 cups) walnut halves, slightly crushed, plus extra to decorate (optional)
525g (1lb 3oz/5¼ cups) ground almonds
2 teaspoons bicarbonate of soda (baking soda)
2 tablespoons ground cinnamon
2 teaspoons allspice
1 teaspoon ground ginger

For the frosting (optional)
300g (11oz/2 cups) cashews, soaked in filtered water for 3–4 hours
2 tablespoons lemon juice
2 tablespoons melted coconut oil
80ml (2¾fl oz/scant ⅓ cup) pure maple syrup

Preheat the oven to 180°C fan/400°F/ Gas 6. Line a 26cm (10in) springform cake tin (pan) with baking paper (parchment paper).

Pour the boiling water over the tea bag in a cup and leave to stand for 10 minutes. Remove the tea bag and set the tea concentrate aside until ready to use.

In a large mixing bowl, beat the eggs together until they are light and fluffy, then add the olive oil, honey, orange zest, masala chai tea and vanilla seeds and whisk generously again until combined.

Now add the carrots and walnuts and mix again. Finally, add the remaining ingredients and mix well to combine everything together.

Pour the mixture into the prepared tin and bake for about 1 hour until risen, golden and a skewer inserted in the centre comes out clean. Remove the cake from the oven and allow to cool completely in the tin. This should take about 2–3 hours.

If you wish to add frosting, use a sharp serrated knife to cut the cake in half horizontally. Wrap the cakes separately in clingfilm (plastic wrap), then chill the cakes for at least 2 hours before frosting.

To make the frosting, blend all the ingredients together in a food processor or blender until smooth. Chill in the refrigerator for 1 hour while the cakes cool before frosting.

Place the bottom cake half on a serving plate. Spread with half of the cashew cream frosting using an offset spatula, if you have one. Place the second cake half over it and spread with the remaining frosting. Decorate with chopped walnuts and serve.

SPICED POACHED PEARS

SERVES 6

6 slightly underripe pears, (peeled)
1 vanilla pod (bean), split in half and
    seeds scraped out
2 cinnamon sticks
2 cloves
4 cardamom pods
1 star anise
4 slices of peeled fresh ginger
1 orange, cut into slices
finely chopped pistachios, to decorate

Place the peeled pears, vanilla pod, spices, ginger and orange slices into a large heavy-based saucepan, then pour in enough filtered water to just cover the pears. Cover the saucepan with a lid and bring to a low simmer. Simmer until the pears are tender. This will depend on how ripe the pears are but generally takes between 30–60 minutes.

Serve with coconut yoghurt or with Chocolate Beetroot Cake (see page 40) sprinkled with chopped pistachios.

CHOCOLATE BEETROOT CAKE

MAKES ONE LARGE 26CM
(10IN) CAKE

I created this dessert when I first began to develop my own dairy-free cakes. A friend gave me the recipe and suggested I try replacing the sugar and flour to create a truly healthy cake... the result is this decadent, wonderfully gooey chocolate cake.

For the cake
600ml (20fl oz/2½ cups) raw honey
600g (1lb/5oz) cooked beetroot
    (beets), puréed in a blender
    or food processor
6 eggs
300ml (10fl oz/1¼ cups) extra virgin
    olive oil
½ vanilla pod (bean), seeds scraped
    out
160g (5½oz/1⅓ cups) raw cacao
    powder
400g (14oz/3 cups) buckwheat flour
4 teaspoons gluten-free baking powder
2 pears, cored and thinly sliced
Spiced Poached Pears (see page 39)

Preheat the oven to 180°C fan/400°F/ Gas 6. Grease a 26cm (10in) springform cake tin (pan), lined with baking paper (parchment paper).

Combine the honey, beetroot purée, eggs, olive oil and vanilla seeds in a large bowl and whisk vigorously to mix the eggs well. Add all the dry ingredients and mix well until smooth.

Pour the mixture into the springform baking tin. Place the pear slices around the edges of the cake and bake for 50–60 minutes or until the middle has risen but still feels a little gooey. Remove from the oven and allow to cool in the tin.

While the cake is in the oven, prepare the poached pears (see page 39) to serve with the cake.

When the cake is ready, remove it from its tin and serve with the poached pear slices. Add a little syrup from the poached pear's saucepan to the cake slices, if desired. Sprinkle the plate with finely chopped pistachios, poached pears (see page 39) and enjoy!

LEMON CHEESECAKE CHIA PUDDING (V)

MAKES 8

This recipe is incredibly filling and packed with clean protein nuts and seeds. Chia seeds also have an abundance of dietary fibre, essential fatty acids and minerals such as calcium for bone health. A diet high in insoluble fibre can help you lose weight, lower cholesterol, and stabilise blood sugar levels, which is especially relevant to the root chakra as it is focused on physical survival.

For the base
400ml (14fl oz) filtered water
1 lemon verbena tea bag
300g (11oz/1⅔ cups) stoned
   (pitted) dates
200g (7oz/1⅓ cups) Brazil nuts,
   roughly chopped

For the filling
150g (5oz/1 cup) cashews, soaked
   in filtered water for 3–4 hours
400ml (14fl oz) can coconut milk
½ vanilla pod (bean), seeds
   scraped out
finely grated zest and juice of
   2 large lemons
12 stoned (pitted) dates
300ml (10fl oz/1¼ cups) filtered water
125g (4oz/generous ¾ cup)
   chia seeds

For the decoration
toasted coconut flakes or dried
   rose petals

To make the base, place the water into a saucepan and add the lemon verbena tea bag. Bring to the boil, then remove the tea bag and add the dates. Reduce the heat to medium and allow the dates to soften in the tea. Using a wooden spoon, begin to stir and break down the dates until a paste is formed. Add the chopped Brazil nuts and stir to combine. Press it into the base of 8 individual glasses or serving dishes.

To make the filling place all the ingredients, except the chia seeds and rose petals, into a blender or food processor and blend on high for at least 2 minutes or until a smooth liquid has formed and all the cashews and dates have been puréed. Pour into a large mixing bowl and add the chia seeds. Use a whisk to make sure all the chia seeds have been evenly distributed into the liquid.

Pour the liquid mixture over the cheesecake base, then place in the refrigerator to chill and set. This will take an hour or you can leave it overnight. Decorate with rose petals or coconut flakes and serve.

Flow

This chapter is based on the second chakra, *svadhisthana,* which means sweetness, and it focuses on strengthening our energy flow, by harnessing the element of water. Water is the ultimate life source of the earth; it makes everything grow, move and change. But water also aids the flow of our human emotions, sensuality and ability to move and shift within our consciousness, which enables us to explore our human meaning and purpose.

The Flow chapter is the core energy source for all movement within our bodies and begins its journey in our reproductive and digestive systems. The ingredients used in this chapter have all been selected to ensure nothing obstructs the flow of energy to these essential organs. This is achieved through simple cooking techniques, such as soaking grains and using fermented foods which replenish our healthy gut bacteria. These flow processes and ingredients result in the nutrients being absorbed more efficiently into our system.

When we feel constricted or obstructed in some way, our flow is limited. The challenge is to find the ability to deal with change and then let it go. It's my belief that the ingredients within this chapter and the energy they create, will help your body to fundamentally let go and flow more freely.

ORANGE & FIG QUINOA BREAKFAST BOWLS (V)

SERVES 4

In nature, seeds are meant to pass through the system of animals relatively undigested so they can be planted elsewhere. To make it possible for seeds to pass through undigested, they contain phytic acids to make them difficult to digest. Seeds also need to be preserved until the time is right for sprouting, so they contain compounds that stop the active enzyme activity of germination. These compounds also serve to hinder active enzyme activity in the digestive system. Beginning the sprouting process, by soaking, makes seeds, grains and nuts more digestible and helps the digestive system obtain all the wonderful nutrients within them.

Prepare this the night before you want to eat it.

200g (7oz/2 cups) quinoa flakes
100g (3½oz/1 cup) quinoa puffs
100g (3½oz/1 cup) gluten-free oats
1 tablespoon vanilla extract
400ml (14fl oz/1¾ cups) freshly
    pressed orange juice (or other juice
    of choice such as apple, carrot or
    pink grapefruit)
150ml (5fl oz/⅔ cup) filtered water,
    plus extra for soaking
10 dried figs, roughly chopped
75g (2½oz/generous ½ cup)
    goji berries
25g (1oz/¼ cup) sunflower seeds
25g (1oz/¼ cup) pumpkin seeds
toasted coconut flakes and fresh fruit,
    (such as figs or blueberries),
    to serve

The evening before, place the quinoa flakes, puffs and oats into a large mixing bowl. Stir to combine, then add the vanilla extract, orange juice and water and stir to combine again. Now add the chopped figs and goji berries and stir well. Cover the bowl with clingfilm (plastic wrap).

Place the seeds in a small bowl and just cover them with filtered water. Cover the bowl with clingfilm. Place both bowls in the refrigerator overnight. They can be kept for 3–5 days in the refrigerator.

In the morning, uncover the soaked quinoa mixture and stir to loosen. You may like to add a little more juice or water to help soften it. Drain the soaked seeds and divide among 4 bowls (or keep the seeds for garnishing the top of the oats). Scoop the soaked quinoa into the bowls, then top with toasted coconut flakes and fresh fruit.

Keeps for 3–5 days in the refrigerator.

VEGGIE BENEDICT WITH TURMERIC HOLLANDAISE

SERVES 2

Breakfast is the most important meal of the day! Our stomachs are at their most active between 7am to 11am. After this, they starts to slow down and digestion takes longer and uses our body's energy less efficiently.

Here is the classic hollandaise with a healthy spin. This recipe re-invents eggs benedict, transforming it into a dairy-free alternative. The combination of cashews and artichokes gives this creamy sauce an amazing texture. Adding a small amount of nutritional yeast to this dish enhances its flavour and creates a rich flavour base.

For the hollandaise sauce

50g (2oz/⅓ cup) raw cashews,
    activated (see page 19)
30g (1oz) canned artichoke heart,
    tough outer leaves removed,
    water reserved
1 tablespoon nutritional yeast
    (or a little miso or tamari soy sauce)
½ teaspoon ground turmeric
pinch of sweet paprika
juice of 1 lemon
½ teaspoon sea salt, or to taste

For the eggs

2 eggs
2 tablespoons distilled white vinegar

For the vegetable layers

2 tablespoons sundried tomato
    pesto (see page 28)
1 ripe avocado, peeled, stoned
    (pitted) and sliced
25g (1oz/½ cup) spinach, washed
    and blanched
8 asparagus spears, trimmed
    and blanched
a little dukkah (optional, see
    page 22), to garnish

For the hollandaise sauce, blend all the ingredients in a high-speed blender or small food processor until completely smooth. If the sauce is too thick, add more reserved artichoke water to reach a desired consistency.

To poach the eggs, heat 4cm (1¾in) water in a deep frying pan over a low heat until just simmering. Add the vinegar and use a wooden spoon to create a whirlpool. Crack each egg into a small mug and then slip into the water. Poach the eggs for 3–4 minutes, then remove with a slotted spoon and drain well.

To assemble, put a spoonful of tomato pesto on each serving plate, then layer avocado slices, blanched spinach and blanched asparagus onto the plates. Top each with a poached egg and a dollop of hollandaise sauce. Sprinkle the plates with a little dukkah, if desired. Serve immediately.

PEA & MINT GLUTEN-FREE SOURDOUGH

SERVES 4

For the sourdough bread

80g (3oz/½ cup) brown
    rice flour
140g (4½oz) cold sourdough
    starter (see opposite page)
460ml (15fl oz/2 cups) filtered
    water at room temperature
20g (¾oz) ground psyllium
    husk
1 tablespoon ground flaxseeds
120g (4oz/scant 1 cup)
    buckwheat flour
60g (2¼oz/½ cup) cornflour
    (cornstarch)
60g (2¼oz/½ cup) potato
    flour (potato starch)
2 tablespoons whole flaxseeds
2 tablespoons sesame seeds
2 tablespoons sunflower seeds
2 tablespoons chia seeds
2 tablespoons coconut sugar
1 teaspoon Himalayan salt

For the pea & mint topping

400g (14oz/2¼ cups) fresh
    shelled or frozen peas
5 sprigs of mint, leaves picked
50ml (1¾fl oz/scant ¼ cup)
    extra-virgin olive oil, plus
    extra to garnish
½ teaspoon sea salt
¼ teaspoon freshly cracked
    black pepper
feta and pomegranate seeds,
    to garnish (optional)

To make the pre-ferment, mix the brown rice flour, sourdough starter and 120ml (4fl oz/½ cup) of the water in a bowl and cover with clingfilm (plastic wrap). Allow to stand for 8–12 hours in a warm, dry place.

In a large mixing bowl, combine 350ml (12fl oz/1⅓ cups) water, the ground psyllium husk and ground flaxseeds and whisk until a thick gel forms. Now add the pre-ferment mixture and incorporate until combined. Ground psyllium seed husks help bind moisture and in bread making helps make the bread less crumbly.

In a separate large bowl, mix all of the remaining ingredients together then make a well in the centre and add the wet pre-ferment and gel mix. Using your hands, work the dough until the flour is fully incorporated. Tip the dough out onto a floured work surface and shape it into your desired loaf shape.

Place the loaf into a bowl lined with a clean tea towel (dishcloth) and dusted with some buckwheat flour to avoid the dough from sticking to the tea towel. Fold the tea towel over the loaf and place the bowl in a plastic bag. Allow to rise in a warm, dry place for 4–6 hours. (The warm switched off oven is my favoured place.) When nearly proved, remove from the oven.

Preheat the oven to 200°C fan/ 430°F/Gas 7. Place a baking tray (baking sheet) on the middle shelf in the oven and then a small baking tin (pan) containing about 1cm (½in) water on the bottom of the oven to heat (this will help the bread form a good crust).

Place a sheet of baking paper (parchment paper) on the work surface. Flip the dough upside down onto the paper and remove the bowl and tea towel. Remove the hot baking tray from the oven and carefully slide the paper with the bread on it onto the baking sheet. Score the bread with a small, sharp knife and return to the oven. Quickly close the oven door and bake for 45 minutes or until the bread is a deep golden colour and the base sounds hollow when tapped. Allow to cool on a wire rack for at least 1 hour before slicing.

To make the topping, bring a saucepan filled with water to the boil. Once boiling, add the peas and blanch briefly. Drain the peas in a colander and run cold water over them, then place them into a food processor along with the mint, oil, salt and pepper. Pulse until a coarse consistency is reached. Taste for seasoning.

To serve, spoon the pea and mint topping onto the toasted sourdough. Using your fingers, crumble a little feta over the top, then sprinkle over some pomegranate seeds and add a drizzle of olive oil.

GLUTEN-FREE SOURDOUGH STARTER

15g (½oz) buckwheat flour
15g (½oz) brown rice flour
2 tablespoons filtered water
10g (¼oz) grated apple
2 tablespoons kefir water
 or previously made
 sourdough starter

Mix all the ingredients in a large, clean glass jar, cover with a muslin cloth and seal it with a rubber band. Place in a dry cupboard away from drafts. Feed the dough 2–3 times a day with 15g (½oz) buckwheat flour, 15g (½oz) brown rice flour and 2 tablespoons water for 7 days. (If the jar gets too full just throw away some of the starter or transfer to a bigger jar. If the sourdough starter separates and liquid starts to form at the top of the starter, pour out the liquid and some of the starter.)

After 7 days, it is ready to use. Store any unused sourdough starter in the refrigerator with the lid on and feed it once a week with the same quantities as before. Remember to feed the dough every time you've used it for baking. For some recipes it can be used cold from the refrigerator (as opposite) but if the recipe calls for an active sourdough starter, remove from the refrigerator and leave it at room temperature for 12 hours before use.

TEMPEH, AVOCADO & THAI SALAD SUMMER ROLLS (V)

MAKES 12

For the Brazil nut dipping sauce
80g (3oz/½ cup) Brazil nuts
1 teaspoon coconut sugar
1 tablespoon coconut paste
1 tablespoon tamari soy sauce
juice of 2 limes
½ teaspoon ground cardamom
1 garlic clove, peeled
1cm (½in) piece of fresh ginger,
    peeled and grated
filtered water

For the salad dressing
pinch of chilli flakes
1 teaspoon grated fresh ginger
4 teaspoons coconut sugar or
    raw honey
2 tablespoons tamari soy sauce
60ml (2fl oz/¼ cup) lime juice
2 tablespoons flaxseed oil

For the Thai salad
60g (2¼oz/⅔ cup) bean sprouts
2 large courgettes (zucchini), spiralised
2 large purple carrots, peeled thinly
½ red (bell) pepper, thinly julienned
¼ red cabbage, thinly sliced
2 spring onions (scallions),
    thinly sliced
bunch of mint, leaves picked
    and roughly chopped
bunch of coriander (cilantro),
    roughly chopped

For the rolls
12 rice paper rounds
small bunch chopped coriander
    (cilantro) leaves
black sesame seeds
1 avocado, peeled, halved,
    stoned (pitted) and cut into
    very thin slices
300g (11oz) cooked tempeh,
    cut into thin strips

To make the dipping sauce, place the nuts, coconut sugar, coconut paste, tamari, lime juice, cardamom, garlic and ginger into a food processor and process until it is a paste. Add a little water to the paste until your desired consistency is reached. Set aside.

To make the salad dressing, place all the ingredients in a bowl and whisk to combine and dissolve the coconut sugar. Set aside.

For the salad, place the ingredients in a large bowl, and toss with some of the dressing until combined.

To make the salad rolls, immerse a rice paper in a bowl of warm water and wait 20–30 seconds for it to soften. Carefully pull it out of the water, holding onto the edges, and immediately spread it out flat on a chopping (cutting) board. To fill the rolls, sprinkle some of the coriander leaves and black sesame seeds over the rice paper, then place 2–3 avocado slices, overlapping each other just to the left of the centre of the rice paper. Place 1–2 pieces of tempeh on top of the avocado, then take a small handful of the dressed salad and place it on top of the tempeh.

You will be able to begin wrapping the roll by folding the left-hand edge of the rice paper over the filling. Tuck it down as far as it can go without breaking the paper, then tuck in the sides of the paper and continue to roll, holding the sides in, until it is closed and snug. Clean the chopping board with kitchen paper (paper towels) continue the process with each rice paper and filling until everything is used. You may need to change the warm water halfway through the process. Cover the paper rolls with damp kitchen paper until ready to serve with the Brazil nut dipping sauce.

ALMOND, BEETROOT & ORANGE PÂTÉ (V)

SERVES 12 AS A SIDE DIP

Nuts create a smooth texture when used in dips such as this one with beetroot (beets) and orange flesh. If you don't have time to activate the nuts, substitute cannellini beans or chickpeas for an instant pâté to serve with roasted vegetables, crackers or an accompaniment to salads.

600g (1lb 6oz) cooked, peeled beetroot (beets), roughly chopped
1 orange, peeled and pips (pits) removed
100g (3½oz/⅔ cup) raw almonds, activated (see page 19)
70g (2½oz/½ cup) raw pistachios, activated (see page 19)
60ml (2fl oz/¼ cup) hemp oil
2 garlic cloves, peeled
1 tablespoon tahini paste
1 teaspoon ground cumin
½ teaspoon Himalayan salt
freshly cracked black pepper

Place all the ingredients into a food processor and blend until smooth. Taste and adjust according to your taste. Store in an airtight container for up to 5 days.

RADISH KIMCHI WITH KALE & BRUSSELS SPROUTS (V)

MAKES ABOUT 900G (2LB)

Kimchi is made by fermenting cabbage with flavourings, a process called lacto-fermentation, in which a salty brine is created to kill all bad bacteria. In turn, *Lactobacillus plantarum* probiotic cells are produced in the final stages of fermentation in both kimchi and sauerkraut.

Kimchi keeps well in the refrigerator. I like to use it as a salad dressing by processing it with an oil of your choice or serve it with simple wok-fried vegetables. However, if you are a real kimchi fiend, grab yourself a spoon and eat it straight from the jar!

500g (1lb 2oz) Brussels sprouts, trimmed
200g (7oz) kale, stalks removed and the leaves roughly torn into pieces
2 teaspoons sea salt
2 tablespoons grated fresh ginger
1 apple, cored and peeled
2–3 garlic cloves, finely chopped
2 tablespoons dried red chilli flakes
2 tablespoons tamari soy sauce
100ml (3½fl oz/scant ½ cup) mushroom stock
4 spring onions (scallions), thinly sliced
1 apple, cored and thinly sliced
10 radishes, washed and sliced
1 tablespoon sesame seeds

Cut each Brussels sprout in half, then place the sprouts and kale into a large mixing bowl. Sprinkle with the salt and toss to combine.

Place the ginger, apple, garlic, chilli flakes and tamari into a food processor and process until the contents become a thick paste. Stop and scrape down the sides of the food processor and then add the mushroom stock and blend.

Add this liquid to the sprout and kale mixture, then use your hands to thoroughly massage the paste into the vegetables. The vegetables should begin to soften and wilt as their liquid is released. Add the spring onions, apple slices, radish slices and sesame seeds and stir to combine.

Pack the now completely combined mixture into a large clean jar, or sealable plastic box, pressing down as you go to eliminate any air. There should be enough liquid to cover the vegetables completely. Place a weight on the vegetables to keep them submerged under the brine. Leave about 2.5cm (1in) space between the kimchi and the top of the container.

Cover the container loosely so air can still escape and place on a plate; it may bubble over while fermenting. Leave at room temperature, ideally between 65–72°C/149-162°F, for 3–5 days. After 3 days, taste the kimchi and press the leaves back down into the brine. If you like the flavour, refrigerate. Otherwise, allow the kimchi to ferment for another couple of days until it reaches the desired tang and kick. Seal and store in the refrigerator for up to 6 months.

BAKED AUBERGINE WITH MISO SATAY (V)

SERVES 4

White miso is made from boiled soybeans, and red miso is made from steamed soybeans. Fermented foods are foods that have been through a process of lacto-fermentation in which natural bacteria feed on the sugar and starch in the food creating lactic acid. This process preserves the food, and creates beneficial enzymes, B-vitamins, Omega-3 fatty acids and various probiotics, improving our digestion. Equally, natural fermentation of foods has been shown to preserve nutrients in food and break it down to a more digestible form.

2 aubergines (eggplants)
1 tablespoon olive oil
sea salt

For the miso satay
80g (3oz/½ cup) cashews, activated (see page 19)
1 tablespoon white miso paste
1 tablespoon tahini paste
1 tablespoon tamarind paste
3 tablespoons tamari soy sauce
1 tablespoon pure maple syrup or coconut nectar
3 tablespoons freshly squeezed orange juice
2.5cm (1in) piece of fresh ginger, peeled
1 large garlic clove, peeled
1 tablespoon olive oil
¼ teaspoon ground coriander
3–4 tablespoons coconut milk (optional), plus 1 tablespoon if needed
toasted black and white sesame seeds, to garnish

Preheat the oven to 200°C fan/425°F/Gas 7. Cut each aubergine in half lengthways. Score across the flesh diagonally one way and then the other to form a diamond pattern (this allows the steam to escape). Drizzle lightly with olive oil, sprinkle with a little sea salt and roast in the oven for 25 minutes until the flesh starts to soften.

While the aubergines are roasting, make the miso satay. Combine all the ingredients with a pinch of salt in a high-speed blender or food processor and process until smooth and thick. Add a little more of the coconut milk, to reach the consistency you desire.

Remove the aubergines from the oven, and spread a layer of the satay sauce over the top of each one. Return to the oven and bake for a further 10 minutes or until the aubergines have become quite gooey. For the last few minutes, turn the oven to its grill (broiler) setting and lightly grill (broil) the top to brown a little. Remove from the grill and allow to cool slightly. Sprinkle a few sesame seeds on each aubergine half and serve.

SUMAC SWEET POTATO, FIG & CHICORY SALAD

SERVES 4

This salad ticks all the yogic boxes. The soft texture of roasted vegetables, the sweetness of fresh fruit, the creamy texture of goat's cheese and the bitterness of chicory (endive) all brought together by a fragrant dressing is healthy and completely delicious.

4 small sweet potatoes, about
    1kg (2¼lb) in total, washed
75ml (2½fl oz/scant ⅓ cup)
    melted coconut oil
1 teaspoon sumac
sea salt and black pepper
4 teaspoons balsamic vinegar
4 teaspoons pure maple syrup
2 teaspoons orange blossom water
2 tablespoons extra-virgin olive oil
2 heads of chicory (Belgian endive),
    trimmed and separated into leaves
100g (3½oz) red chard leaves,
    washed or baby spinach leaves
4 spring onions (scallions), thinly
    sliced on the angle
6 fresh, ripe figs
150g (5oz/⅔ cup) soft goat's
    cheese, crumbled

Preheat the oven to 220°C fan/475°F/Gas 9. Line 2 baking trays (baking sheets) with baking paper (parchment paper). Cut the sweet potato into wedges by halving them lengthways and then cutting each half into 3–5 long wedges.

Place the sweet potato wedges into a large mixing bowl, sprinkle with the coconut oil, sumac and a little salt and pepper. Toss to combine, then spread the wedges out onto the prepared baking trays, skin side down, and cook for 25 minutes until soft and browned. Remove from the oven and allow to cool.

To make the dressing, whisk together the balsamic vinegar, maple syrup, orange blossom water, olive oil and salt and pepper in a small jug (pitcher). Set aside.

Mix the sweet potatoes, chicory leaves, red chard and spring onions (scallions) together in a large mixing bowl. Place the salad on a large serving platter, then rip the figs into pieces and dot over the top. Scatter the crumbled goat's cheese over, and drizzle a little of the dressing over the salad.

Serve at room temperature with a little more dressing, if desired.

GET THE GLOW JUICE (V)

SERVES 2

This truly is a healing juice. Banish those creaky joints, stiff muscles, cramps and circulation problems with this juice. The anti-cancer, antioxidant, anti-inflammatory and strengthening benefits of turmeric are what makes this juice glow with health. Additionally, carrots' ability to strengthen the stomach, liver and lungs, and sweet potatoes' capacity to regulate blood sugar levels, means that this juice will breathe new life into any sore or tired body.

½ sweet potato, peeled
2 carrots, thoroughly scrubbed but not peeled
1 yellow or red (bell) pepper
1 lime, peeled
1cm (½in) piece of fresh turmeric (or ½ teaspoon ground turmeric)

Pass all the ingredients through a juicer and serve.

SACRAL SAVIOUR JUICE (V)

SERVES 2

Fennel contains compounds known as phytoestrogens, these are plant chemicals that are similar in chemical structure to the female hormone oestrogen. These compounds are known to be of great use for conditions where a change in oestrogen levels cause symptoms, such as the menopause or pre-menstrual issues. Also it has been found to help release endorphins into the bloodstream. These 'feel-good' chemicals create a mood of euphoria and it is thought they may help relieve depression associated with certain illnesses as well as dampen anxiety.

2 large fennel bulbs, with green fronds
2 Bartlett (or other seasonal) pears
2.5cm (1in) piece of fresh ginger
4 sprigs of mint
2 tablespoons aloe vera juice

Pass the fennel, pears, ginger and mint through a juicer, then stir in the aloe vera juice and serve.

Pictured L–R (see opposite): Sacral Saviour Juice and Get the Glow Juice

CLEMENTINE & PASSION FRUIT REJUVELAC FLOAT (V)

SERVES 2

Rejuvelac may have an odd name, but this drink can give you a healthy energy boost, improve your digestion and give you a probiotic and vitamin B complex hit, including vitamin B12. Rejuvelac is a non-alcoholic, fermented liquid made from sprouted grains. You can easily make it yourself or just pick up a bottle from a shop. When it's done, the liquid should be yellowish, cloudy, slightly sweet and tart but not too sour. It will also be slightly carbonated, with a hint of lemon. You can choose to sprout any grain; I chose quinoa because it doesn't take long to sprout – about 24 hours. You do need to allow several days to make the rejuvelac though as it needs time to ferment.

For the rejuvelac
200g (7oz/1 cup) quinoa
1.5 litres (50fl oz/6¼ cups) filtered
    water

For the float
200ml (7fl oz/scant 1 cup) freshly
    pressed clementine juice
Coconut, Ginger & Miso Ice Cream
    (see page 157)
2 passion fruits, seeds scooped out

To make the rejuvelac, place the quinoa into a non-reactive sieve (strainer) and rinse well in cold running water. Tip into a large bowl and pour in enough filtered water to cover. Leave to soak for 12 hours.

In the morning, tip the quinoa back into the sieve and rinse. Cover lightly with a towel and leave to sprout. It usually takes 24 hours to sprout at room temperature. Rinse and drain a few times during that time, keeping the grain moist but not wet.

Once the quinoa has sprouted, rinse and place into a 1 litre jar (34fl oz/4¼ cups), and fill the jar with the measured water. Store the jar in a warm place out of direct sunlight for 2 days, stirring the contents of the jar at least once a day. When the rejuvelac is ready, the water will turn cloudy and white. Strain the liquid into clean bottles and discard the quinoa. The cloudy white liquid is your rejuvelac. Store in the refrigerator for up to 1 week, it will sweeten with time.

To make the float, mix 60ml (2fl oz/1¼ cups) of the rejuvelac liquid with the clementine juice. Take 2 serving glasses and place a scoop of the ice-cream at the bottom of the glass. Now pour the juice mixture over the top of the ice-cream and wait for the ice-cream to float and bubble.

Spoon the passion fruit seeds over the top and serve immediately with a straw and long serving spoon.

SILKY GREEN TEA, LIME & AVOCADO MOUSSE (V)

SERVES 2

If there was one food I could not live without, or consider more well rounded, it would be the avocado. Just one avocado contains 40% of your daily fibre, 30% of your daily potassium and 30% of your daily folate needs.

As a source of fat, they're not only a rich source of oleic acid (Omega-3 fatty acids), they also lower bad LDL cholesterol and raise good HDL cholesterol. This silky flesh, helps to re-establish hormonal balance, depresses insulin production, maintains clear smooth skin, stabilises energy levels and is a rich source of digestive enzymes.

flesh of 2 small or 1 large, ripe avocado
     (about 250g/9oz flesh)
finely grated zest and juice of 2 limes
50g (2oz) raw honey or coconut nectar
50ml (1¾fl oz/scant ¼ cup) melted
     coconut oil
½ teaspoon matcha powder
pistachios, finely chopped
     to decorate

Place the avocado flesh, lime zest and juice, honey or coconut nectar, coconut oil and matcha powder into a blender or food processor and blend together until fully combined and smooth.

Transfer the mixture to 2 serving dishes of your choice. Cover with clingfilm (plastic wrap) and place in the refrigerator to allow to firm for about 1 hour.

When ready to serve, sprinkle over the pistachio crumbs and enjoy the smooth indulgence. (This mousse should be eaten on the same day before the avocado starts to discolour.)

CINNAMON YOGHURT BARK WITH STRAWBERRIES

SERVES 6

The types of bacteria in our intestines have a profound effect on our health. Good bacteria are anti-inflammatory, whereas bad bacteria secrete highly inflammatory substances into the gut. The word probiotic literally means to promote life. The term is used to describe living microorganisms in the intestines that have positive health effects. Along with regularly eating fermented foods, consuming unflavoured, sugar-free, natural yoghurt is an excellent way to increase your healthy bacteria. Flavour the yoghurt in any way you want, I've roasted the strawberries, which increases their flavour, while the addition of balsamic vinegar diffuses their sweetness.

For the yoghurt bark
500g (1lb oz/2¼ cups) full-fat natural yoghurt or Greek yoghurt
4 tablespoons pure maple syrup
½ teaspoon ground cinnamon
2 tablespoons vanilla extract
200g (7oz/2⅓ cups) fresh blueberries, or blackberries if blueberries are unavailable, stray stems removed
25g (1oz/⅙ cup) cacao nibs
50g (2oz/⅓ cup) raw pistachios, roughly chopped, plus a few extra for scattering over serving plates

For the roasted strawberries
500g (1lb 2oz/3⅓ cups) fresh strawberries, washed and quartered
2 tablespoons vanilla extract
1 tablespoon balsamic vinegar
1 tablespoon filtered water

Line a 20 x 20cm (8 x 8in) shallow baking tin (pan) with baking paper (parchment paper). In a medium bowl, stir together the yoghurt, maple syrup, cinnamon and vanilla. Gently stir in the blueberries and cacao nibs and mix until everything is combined. Pour the mixture into the tin, spreading it out evenly, making sure the blueberries are evenly distributed. Sprinkle the chopped pistachios over the yoghurt surface. Cover with clingfilm (plastic wrap) and place in the freezer overnight or until required.

On the day of serving (you still need to be working ahead of time as the mixture needs time to cool), preheat the oven to 160°C fan/350°F/ Gas 4. Place the strawberries in a glass baking dish and spread out in an even layer. In a small bowl, stir the vanilla, balsamic vinegar and water together. Pour this mixture over the strawberries and place in the oven for 20 minutes or until the strawberries are tender and cooked. Remove from the oven and allow to cool.

Drain the liquid from the strawberries into a small saucepan. Bring to the boil until reduced to a thickened sauce. Leave to cool.

When ready to serve, spread a little of the strawberry sauce over 6 serving plates and add the roasted strawberries with the yoghurt bark. Scatter a few chopped pistachios over the top and serve immediately.

CHOCOLATE & MACA QUINOA POPS (V)

MAKES 12 BARS

The sacral chakra is associated with emotions, desire and sexuality. Desire is an emotional impulse that inspires us to move to something greater; to embrace change. If we don't desire anything, the senses shut down and we lose our ability to expand.

The herb, maca, can help. It is known as an adaptogen. Adaptogens are special kinds of herbs that adjust to a variety of conditions within the body and help restore it to a healthy balance. Maca, in particular, works on the endocrine system to balance hormones in both men and women, increasing sexual desire. Safe to use daily, maca can be added to many recipes such as these chocolate pops or your morning smoothies. These bars are best eaten from the refrigerator. Other puffed grains can be used such as millet or buckwheat.

120ml (4fl oz/½ cup) melted
   coconut oil
120ml (4fl oz/½ cup) coconut nectar,
   raw honey or pure maple syrup
60g (2¼oz/½ cup) cacao powder
40g (1½oz) maca powder
pinch of salt
80g (3oz/1½ cups) puffed quinoa
   (or other puffed cereals such
   as rice, spelt, buckwheat, millet)
80g (3oz/½ cup) roasted hazelnuts,
   roughly chopped
40g (1½oz/⅓ cup) dried unsweetened
   cranberries, roughly chopped
40g (1½oz/¼ cup) raw pistachios,
   roughly chopped

Place the coconut oil in a medium saucepan over a medium–low heat. Add the 2 tablespoons of sweetener of your choice and combine. Now add the cacao and maca powder, plus the pinch of salt and whisk until the mixture forms a loose paste. Remove from the heat.

Add the quinoa puffs, and stir to combine, making sure all the ingredients are coated in the chocolate paste. Taste and add a little more salt if needed.

Line a 15 x 20cm (6 x 8in) baking tin (pan) with baking paper (parchment paper) and scoop the batter into it. Use the palm of your hands to press everything loosely down into the tin.

Now sprinkle the hazelnuts, cranberries and pistachios evenly over the surface and, using the palm of your hands again, press everything together tightly and evenly to roughly 2–3cm (¾–1in) deep. Leave to cool, then place in the refrigerator to firm for 30 minutes.

These bars will last for 1 week in the refrigerator, or can be frozen for up to 2 months.

Vitalise

This chapter is based on the third chakra known as the solar plexus, *manipura*. The purpose of the third chakra is to transform the matter of the first chakra and the energy of the second chakra into a conscious direction of activity. It's in this chakra that our energy systems come into play.

Our adrenal health (our ability to respond to stress) is a crucial element in maintaining a balanced energy system and we can maintain it through our diets; this is achieved by the reduction or elimination of simple carbohydrates, replacing them instead with complex carbohydrates containing both fibre and starch. These are both then converted into energy within the body, which is slowly released over a longer period of time and ensures we maintain our energy stores and adrenal health.

The recipes in this chapter have been designed to showcase some of the best foods to help you feel satisfied and energised for the whole day. The recipes feature carbohydrates such as sweet potato, legumes, chickpeas, oats and other whole grains. This chapter also focuses on naturally metabolism-boosting foods, such as cinnamon, almonds and spinach as well as fiery, energetic foods such as turmeric, ginger and chilli. They are not only highly nutritious, complex carbohydrates but are also awesome at maintaining healthy energy stores.

PICK-ME-UP LIQUORICE TOFFEE (V)

MAKES 14 SQUARES

Liquorice is one of my favourite herbs. I use it as an adrenal tonic specifically, but there are also many studies showing its effect on the endocrine system. Liquorice contains plant oestrogens (phytoestrogens) and helps to lower the amount of testosterone (the male hormone) in women. This is particularly useful for treating conditions such as polycystic ovaries or where there is menstrual irregularities. Liquorice is a powerful herb and I advise not to eat more than 50g (2oz) liquorice per day.

300g (11oz/2½ cups) stoned (pitted) prunes
40ml (1½oz/scant ¼ cup) melted coconut oil
40g (1½oz/scant ½ cup) ground almonds
2 teaspoons carob powder (optional)
2 teaspoons raw liquorice powder plus extra for dusting
¼ teaspoon ground star anise
½ teaspoon Himalayan salt

Place all the ingredients into a food processor and blend thoroughly until a smooth, fudge-like dough is formed. This may take up to 5 minutes.

Remove the dough from the food processor and press firmly into a 20 x 20cm (8 x 8in) square baking tray (baking sheet), lined with baking paper (parchment paper). Dust with a little extra liquorice powder and refrigerate for 1 hour.

Once cooled, remove from the refrigerator and lift the baking paper out of the tray. Cut the toffee into equal squares and enjoy when you need that little pick-me-up.

MACA & LACUMA POPCORN (V)

SERVES 4

Maca and lacuma have become popular superfoods for their sweet and palatable flavour. Particularly useful for increasing energy, endurance and stamina, balancing hormones and increasing fertility, Maca is an athlete's best friend. Perfect for snacking time.

120ml (4fl oz/½ cup) coconut oil
200g (7oz/scant 1 cup) popping corn kernels
½ teaspoon fine Himalayan salt
2 tablespoons maca powder
2 tablespoons lacuma powder

Pour the coconut oil into a large heavy-based saucepan. Drop 4 kernels into the bottom of the pan, cover with a lid and place over a medium–high heat. Once the few kernels pop, add the rest of the kernels to the saucepan, replace the lid and remove from the heat for 30 seconds. Return the saucepan to the heat and wait for the popping to begin. Shake the pan vigorously a few times. Once the popping slows remove from the heat and allow to cool, then uncover. Tip the popped corn into a large serving bowl and sprinkle the salt, maca and lacuma powders over the popcorn and toss to coat each kernel.

Pictured L–R (text on opposite page): Pick-Me-Up Liquorice Toffee and Maca & Lacuma Popcorn

OAT GRANOLA

SERVES 12

500g (1lb 2oz/5 cups) gluten-free
  rolled oats
200g (7oz/2 cups) quinoa flakes
200g (7oz/1¼ cups) raw almonds
200g (7oz/1¼ cups) raw hazelnuts
200g (7oz/1⅔ cups) pumpkin seeds
200g (7oz/1⅔ cups) sunflower seeds
100g (3½oz/generous ¾ cup)
  flaxseeds
150g (5oz/1¼ cups) dried cranberries
150g (5oz/1¼ cups) sultanas
  (golden raisins)
2 teaspoons ground cinnamon
1 tablespoon vanilla extract
500g (1lb 2oz/scant 1½ cups)
  raw honey
400ml (14fl oz/¾ cups) extra-virgin
  olive oil

Preheat the oven to 160°C fan/350°F/
Gas 4. Line 3 baking trays (baking
sheets) with baking paper (parchment
paper). Combine all the dry ingredients
in a large mixing bowl.

Place the vanilla, honey and
olive oil into a saucepan and heat
gently until the honey melts and the
mixture is runny. This will help to
distribute the mixture evenly through
the dry ingredients. Remove from
the heat.

Pour the honey mixture over the
dry ingredients and stir thoroughly to
combine. Transfer the granola to the
prepared baking trays and spread out
evenly. The baking trays should only
have 2cm (¾in) thin layer of granola.
Bake for 35 minutes or so, until the
granola is deep golden brown.

Remove from the oven and allow to
cool completely on the baking trays.
The granola should be dry and not
sticky. If sticky the granola should be
cooked at the same temperature for
another 10 minutes but be careful not
to let it burn.

The key to this granola keeping its
characteristic clumps is to not touch
or move the granola at any stage of its
baking or cooling process.

Once cooled, the granola can be
stored in an airtight container. Break
up the granola clumps with your
fingers as needed.

BANANA, ALMOND & CHIA BREAD WITH COCONUT YOGHURT

SERVES 10

An interesting fact about bananas is that their nutrient profile changes as they ripen. Japanese researchers have shown that the antioxidant and anticancer properties of the banana surge as it ripens. An overripe banana which has dark patches on its yellow skin produce a substance called TNF (Tumour Necrosis Factor), which has the ability to combat abnormal cancer cells. So, the more dark patches the banana has, the higher its immunity enhancement properties.

For the banana bread
450g (1lb/generous 2 cups) mashed, overripe bananas
5 eggs
90g (3¼oz/¼ cup) raw honey
90ml (3fl oz/⅓ cup) extra-virgin olive oil
2 teaspoons vanilla extract
1 teaspoon ground cinnamon
1 teaspoon gluten-free baking powder
2 tablespoons lemon juice
300g (11oz/3 cups) ground almonds
30g (1oz/3 tablespoons) chia seeds
1 just-ripe banana, peeled

For the whipped coconut yoghurt
300g (11oz/1¼ cups) coconut yoghurt
85g (3oz/⅓ cup) raw honey, plus extra for drizzling
1 teaspoon ground cinnamon
½ vanilla pod (bean), seeds scraped out

Preheat the oven to 160°C fan/350°F/Gas 4. Line a 30 x 10cm (12 x 4in) loaf tin (pan) with baking paper (baking parchment). In a large mixing bowl, combine the mashed bananas, eggs, honey, oil, vanilla, cinnamon, baking powder and lemon juice. (The lemon juice will activate the baking powder.) Now add the ground almonds and chia seeds and mix well.

Spoon the batter into the prepared loaf tin. For decoration, cut the extra banana in half lengthways and then place, cut sides up, on top of the batter. Bake in the oven on the middle shelf for an hour.

This is a very moist loaf, a skewer may not come out completely clean, but if the centre feels firm then remove from the oven and allow to cool completely before turning out and removing the baking paper.

To make the whipped coconut yoghurt, place the yoghurt into a food processor along with the honey, cinnamon and vanilla seeds and blend until thick and creamy.

To serve, place slices of banana bread under a hot grill (broiler). Once browned, remove from the grill and place on serving plates along with a dollop of whipped coconut yoghurt and a drizzle of honey.

ZA'ATAR SPICED CHICKPEA CRACKERS (V)

MAKES 32 CRACKERS

For the za'atar

1 tablespoon fresh oregano, finely chopped (or 1 teaspoon dried oregano)

1 tablespoon fresh marjoram, finely chopped (or 1 teaspoon dried marjoram)

1 tablespoon sumac

1 tablespoon ground cumin

1 teaspoon toasted fennel seeds

1 tablespoon toasted sesame seeds

1 teaspoon sea salt

1 teaspoon freshly cracked black pepper

For the crackers

350g (12oz/3¼ cups) chickpea (garbanzo or besan) flour

1 teaspoon sea salt

1 teaspoon gluten-free baking powder

2 tablespoons extra-virgin olive oil, plus extra for coating

75ml (2½fl oz/scant ⅓ cup) warm filtered water

sea salt flakes, to garnish

To make the za'atar, preheat the oven to 180°C fan/400°F/Gas 6. If using fresh herbs, place the thyme and marjoram leaves on a baking tray (baking sheet) and place in the oven for 10 minutes.

Use a mortar and pestle to grind the oregano and marjoram leaves finely. Remove any 'woody' pieces. Now add the sumac, cumin, fennel and sesame seeds, sea salt and black pepper and give another quick crush to combine. Set aside in a small bowl.

Next, make the crackers. In a large bowl, mix the flour, salt and baking powder together. Using your hands, rub the oil into the flour for a few minutes to distribute it evenly with no lumps. Gradually work in the warm water until the mixture forms a ball (if the dough is still a little dry, add more water). Turn out onto a lightly floured surface and knead for 5 minutes. (Alternatively, place the flour, salt and baking powder in a food processor with the dough hook. Add the olive oil and process briefly, then with the machine running, gradually trickle in the warm water until the mixture forms a dough ball. Continue to run the machine for 1 minute to knead the dough.)

Divide the dough in half and wrap in clingfilm (plastic wrap) forming a disc like-shape. Leave to rest for 15 minutes.

While the dough is resting, preheat the oven again to 180°C fan/400°F/Gas 6 and line 2 baking trays (baking sheets) with baking paper (parchment paper). Then prepare a flat surface with 2 pieces of baking paper.

Place one piece of dough on top of one piece of baking paper then, with wet hands, slightly flatten the dough with your palm. Cover the dough with a second piece of baking paper and roll the dough until it is roughly 3–4mm (1–1½in) thick. Remove the top paper and trim the edges square with a knife. Place on a baking tray and repeat the process.

Sprinkle the dough with a little za'atar, then gently roll the rolling pin over the dough again to push the za'atar into the dough. Using a pastry brush, lightly brush the tops of the dough squares with olive oil, then sprinkle with salt. Using a sharp knife or pizza cutter, cut out crackers in your desired shape (squares are easiest) and transfer to baking trays.

Bake for 15–20 minutes. The crackers are cooked when slightly browned. Allow to cool on the baking trays and store in an airtight container.

MUHAMMARA

(V)   SERVES 4–6

This stuff is seriously
addictive! Serve it with
Za'atar Spiced Chickpea
Crackers (see opposite page).

4 red (bell) peppers, washed
90ml (3fl oz/⅓ cup) extra-
    virgin olive oil, plus extra
    for drizzling
2 garlic cloves, peeled
90g (3¼oz/¾ cup) raw walnuts
100g (3½oz/scant ½ cup)
    chickpeas (garbanzos),
    cooked and drained
handful of fresh coriander
    (cilantro)
2 tablespoons pomegranate
    molasses
juice of 1 lemon
1 teaspoon ground cumin
1 teaspoon sumac
½ teaspoon chilli (chili) flakes
1 teaspoon Himalayan salt
freshly cracked black pepper

Pictured L–R: Muhammara and Za'atar Spiced Chickpea Crackers (text on page opposite)

Preheat oven to 220°C fan/475°F/Gas
9. Line a baking tray (baking sheet)
with baking paper (parchment paper).

Place the peppers onto the baking
tray and lightly drizzle with a little of
the olive oil. Roast for 20 minutes or
until the peppers are soft and the skin
has blistered. You may like to turn
the oven to the grill (broiler) setting
and finish the peppers off by grilling
(broiling) the skins to add a little
charcoal flavour.

Once roasted, remove the peppers
from the oven, then immediately place
into a bowl and cover with clingfilm
(plastic wrap). This will help loosen

the skins away from the flesh,
making the peppers easier to
peel. After 10 minutes, remove the
clingfilm from the bowl and using
your fingers, begin to peel the skins
and seeds away from the flesh.

Discard the stalks and seeds
then place the flesh of the roasted
peppers into a food processor with
the garlic and process until smooth.
Add the rest of the ingredients
and blend again until a smooth
consistency is reached.

Taste the muhammara for
seasoning and serve with a drizzle
of olive oil on top.

HIGH-JACKED SWEET POTATO WITH AVOCADO, POMEGRANATE & COCONUT (V)

SERVES 2

Switch your white potatoes for sweet potatoes because they are filled with unbelievable vitamins. This recipe makes for the perfect lunch.

2 sweet potatoes (about 180g/6oz total weight)
50ml (1¾fl oz/scant ¼ cup) melted coconut oil
½ red onion, thinly sliced
80g (3oz/generous ½ cup) cooked black beans, rinsed and drained
50g (2oz/1 cup) spinach leaves, washed
½ teaspoon ground cumin
sea salt and freshly cracked black pepper
flesh of ½ avocado, diced
1 tablespoon toasted unsweetened coconut flakes
2 tablespoons torn coriander (cilantro) leaves
20g (¾oz/½ cup) rocket (arugula) leaves, washed
¼ pomegranate, seeds only
sea salt flakes
2 lime wedges

Preheat the oven to 200°C/430°F/Gas 7. Using a small sharp knife, pierce each sweet potato a few times. Place the sweet potatoes on a baking tray (baking sheet) lined with baking paper (parchment paper). Bake in the oven for about 50 minutes, or until the sweet potatoes feel tender when squeezed. Remove from the oven and allow to cool a little.

While the sweet potatoes are baking, place 2 tablespoons of the coconut oil in a large frying pan over a medium–high heat. Add the onion and sauté until fragrant. Turn down the heat to medium–low and cook for a further 15 minutes or until soft and caramelised. Add the black beans, spinach and cumin and season with salt and pepper. Mix gently and cook for a further minute or until the spinach has just begun to wilt and the beans are warmed through.

To serve, cut a slit through the top of the sweet potatoes and push the sides of the skin down so the cooked potato is exposed a little. Season the potato with salt and pepper and ½ tablespoon of coconut oil on each. Top with the black bean spinach mixture then add the rocket, top with diced avocado, coconut flakes, coriander leaves, rocket leaves, pomegranate seeds, sea salt flakes, black pepper and a wedge of lime to squeeze over.

BEETROOT & LENTIL PANZANELLA SALAD

SERVES 2

For the salad

80g (3oz/scant ½ cup) Puy lentils, washed and drained
½ teaspoon vegetable stock powder
2 small raw beetroot (beets), scrubbed
8 baby turnips, with leaves still attached, scrubbed (or use large radishes when turnips not in season)
1 tablespoon raw honey
2 tablespoons melted coconut oil
sea salt and freshly cracked black pepper
gluten-free sourdough bread, torn into small pieces (see page 50)
2 eggs
125g (4oz/2¼ cups) halloumi
50g (2oz/1 cup) baby red chard leaves, washed
2 tablespoons Almond, Beetroot & Orange Pâté (see page 53)

For the tahini dressing

juice of 1 lime
1 tablespoon tahini paste
2 tablespoons olive oil
pinch of sea salt
pinch of ground coriander

Preheat the oven to 180°C fan/400°F/Gas 6. Begin by cooking the lentils. Bring a large saucepan of water to the boil, add the vegetable stock powder and allow to dissolve, then add the lentils and cook for about 15 minutes or until tender but still with some texture. Drain and return to the pan.

While the lentils are cooking, quarter the beetroot and place on a baking tray (baking sheet) lined with baking paper (parchment paper) with the baby turnips. Drizzle the honey, 1 teaspoon of the coconut oil, salt and pepper over the top and toss to coat.

Roast for about 15 minutes or until tender and cooked through. Remove from the oven and set aside.

Meanwhile, heat the remaining coconut oil in a non-stick frying pan, add the sourdough bits and toss in the oil to coat. Tip them onto a baking tray and spread out. Place in the oven for 5–8 minutes while the vegetables are cooking to crisp and brown then remove from the oven and set aside.

Boil the eggs in a small saucepan for 4 minutes, then remove with a slotted spoon and allow to cool under cold running water for a minute. Carefully peel, then set aside.

Reheat the same frying pan you used to toss the bread, crumble in the halloumi and gently brown on all sides. This will only take a few minutes. Remove from the pan and set aside.

To make the tahini dressing, whisk together the lime, tahini, oil, salt and ground coriander. Add to the cooked lentils and toss. Now add the sourdough pieces and baby red chard leaves and toss once again.

Serve the salad with halloumi crumbs and a dollop of the Almond, Beetroot & Orange Paté. Place an egg on the plate and just before serving, break the egg, so that the yolk begins to run. Serve immediately.

COCONUT CURRY PUMPKIN SOUP (V)

SERVES 6–8

650g (1lb 7oz) pumpkin, peeled, seeded and chopped into large chunks
50ml (1¾fl oz/scant ¼ cup) melted coconut oil
sea salt and freshly cracked black pepper
1 large red onion, coarsely chopped
4 garlic cloves, peeled
1 stem lemongrass
2 tablespoons Thai red curry paste
2 teaspoons grated fresh ginger
1 litre (34fl oz/4¼ cups) vegetable stock
400ml (14fl oz) can coconut milk
2 tablespoons pure maple syrup
juice of 1 lime

Preheat the oven to 200°C fan/430°F/ Gas 7. Line a baking tray (baking sheet) with baking paper (parchment paper). Place the pumpkin chunks onto the prepared baking tray and drizzle with 2 tablespoons of the coconut oil and some salt and pepper. Roast in the oven for 30–40 minutes or until tender and cooked through. Remove from the oven and set aside.

Now sauté the onion in 2 tablespoons of the coconut oil in a large saucepan over a medium heat, until soft and translucent. Add the garlic cloves, lemongrass, curry paste and ginger, cook for a further 2–3 minutes or until fragrant.

Now add the pumpkin and mix everything together. Break the pumpkin pieces down with a wooden spoon but before things start sticking to the bottom of the saucepan, add the vegetable stock. Allow the soup to come back to the boil, then remove from the heat. Leave to cool for 5–10 minutes then add the coconut milk, maple syrup and lime juice. Using a hand-held blender, purée the soup until smooth. Taste and adjust the seasoning to your liking.

VELVET WHITE BEAN RISOTTO (V)

SERVES 6

Risotto is one of my all-time favourite dishes for when I need to feel warm and full. I have substituted the Arborio rice from a traditional risotto for cannellini beans for added fibre and flavour. This recipe is deliciously creamy yet light as the lemon zest added at the end lifts the entire dish.

500ml (17fl oz/2¼ cups) vegetable stock
50ml (1¾fl oz/scant ¼ cup) coconut oil
1 brown onion, finely chopped
2 garlic cloves, finely chopped
2 leeks, trimmed and sliced
500g (1lb 2oz/3¼ cups) frozen broad (fava) beans
2 x 400g (14oz) cans cannellini beans (or any white beans such as haricot), drained
250g (9oz/5 cups) spinach leaves
finely grated zest and juice of 1 lemon, plus extra to garnish
3 sprigs of thyme, leaves picked, plus extra to garnish
Himalayan salt and freshly cracked black pepper

Bring the vegetable stock to a simmer in a saucepan over a medium heat and set aside.

Heat the coconut oil in a large saucepan over a medium heat. Add the onion, garlic and leeks and gently sauté for 5–8 minutes or until translucent, stirring occasionally. Add 225ml (8fl oz/1 cup) of the stock and cook, stirring until almost absorbed. Now add the broad beans, cannellini beans and the remaining stock. Cook, stirring for a couple of minutes until hot through, then add the spinach leaves and allow to wilt. Add the lemon juice, zest and thyme leaves.

Remove from the heat and season with salt, pepper and more thyme if needed. Serve immediately sprinkled with some extra grated lemon zest and thyme leaves before serving.

SWEET POTATO GNOCCHI WITH WALNUT PESTO & SAGE

SERVES 4

For the walnut pesto
400g (14oz/4 cups) fresh, shelled walnuts or raw ready-shelled walnuts if unavailable
1 garlic clove, peeled
6 tablespoons extra-virgin olive oil
½ teaspoon sea salt

For the gnocchi
200g (7oz) boiled sweet potatoes, puréed
300g (11oz/1¼ cups) chestnut purée
½ teaspoon Himalayan salt
½ teaspoon ground nutmeg
250g (9oz/2 cups) chestnut flour (or buckwheat flour if unavailable)
2 eggs
rice flour, for dusting

For the topping
2 tablespoons melted coconut oil
leaves from 2 sprigs of sage
extra-virgin olive oil

To make the walnut pesto, preheat oven to 170°C fan/375°F/Gas 5. Place the shelled walnuts onto a baking tray (baking sheet) and roast in the oven until just golden. This should take 4–5 minutes. Remove from the oven and wrap the walnuts in a clean tea towel (dishcloth) and rub them together to remove their skins.

Place the walnuts into a food processor along with the garlic, oil and salt and blend until smooth, adding a little more oil if needed to make a thick pouring consistency.

Now make the gnocchi. Using the dough hook of your food processor, blend the sweet potato and chestnut purées, until combined, then add salt, nutmeg and a little of the chestnut flour at a time. Add the eggs, one at a time and process until a dough is formed. The dough should be soft and elastic. If the dough is too sticky or dry add a little water or flour. (You can also mix it with a wooden spoon in a large bowl.)

Divide the dough into 6 even portions. Wrap in clingfilm (plastic wrap) and refrigerate for 30 minutes. Remove from the refrigerator and knead gently on a surface dusted with rice flour. Roll the dough into long, thin cylinders, about 1cm (½in) thick, then cut the cylinders into 2cm (¾in) pieces. Roll each piece in rice flour, shaking off any excess. Now roll the pieces over a gnocchi board or press with a fork.

Bring a saucepan of salted water to the boil. Once boiling, reduce the heat to a simmer and add half of the gnocchi. In about 5–8 minutes, when the gnocchi have started to float to the top, cook them for a further minute. Remove to a plate using a slotted spoon and repeat the process with the second batch of gnocchi. Coat the gnocchi in the walnut pesto and spoon into warmed shallow serving bowls with a drizzle of olive oil.

Quickly heat 2 tablespoons coconut oil in a frying pan over a medium heat, and add the sage leaves once the oil is very hot. The sage leaves should crisp and go bright green quickly. Remove from the pan with a slotted spoon and drain on kitchen paper. Serve over the gnocchi.

ONE-POT MASALA DHAL (V)

SERVES 2

This fragrant dhal is a real crowd-pleaser. Smooth and creamy in texture, the use of red lentils means this dhal can be ready and enjoyed much quicker than when using other varieties of lentils. You can even substitute with ready-cooked chickpeas for an even faster on-the-go meal. Extra paste can be kept in an airtight container.

For the masala paste

1½ teaspoons cumin seeds
1½ teaspoons coriander seeds
2cm (¾in) piece of fresh ginger, peeled and cut into thin slices
1 teaspoon chilli flakes
1 tablespoon smoked paprika
2 teaspoons garam marsala
1 teaspoon Himalayan salt
2 tablespoons melted coconut oil
2 tablespoons tomato purée (paste)
bunch of coriander (cilantro) leaves

For the dhal

1 tablespoon coconut oil
1 small red onion, finely diced
2 garlic cloves, finely chopped
3 tablespoons masala paste (see above)
160g (5½oz/generous ¾ cup) chopped tomatoes
400ml (14fl oz/1¾ cups) coconut milk
100g (3½oz/generous ⅓ cup) red lentils
50g (2oz/1 cup) spinach
coriander leaves and Greek yoghurt, to garnish

To make the masala paste, toast the cumin and coriander seeds in a frying pan until fragrant, then place in a mortar and pestle and grind them together.

Tip them into a small food processor, add the ginger, chilli flakes, smoked paprika, garam masala, and salt and pulse a few times to incorporate. Next, add the coconut oil, tomato purée and coriander leaves and pulse again until a smooth paste forms. Set aside.

To make the curry, heat a large frying pan over a medium heat. Add the coconut oil and onion and sauté for 4–5 minutes until translucent. Add the garlic and cook for a further minute. Stir in the masala paste and cook for a further 1–2 minutes, stirring. Now add the chopped tomatoes and coconut milk, stirring everything together. Taste a little of the sauce and add a little more masala paste if needed. Bring to the boil. Add the lentils and reduce the heat to medium–low. Give the curry a stir every now and then until the lentils are tender, about 20–25 minutes.

Remove from the heat and fold in the spinach. Season with salt and pepper and serve garnished with coriander leaves and a dollop of Greek yoghurt.

CREAMY BANANA WARRIOR SMOOTHIE

SERVES 2

The sprinkling of LSA mix over the top is something I have done for many years. LSA is a mix of ground flaxseeds, sunflower seeds and almonds. This healthy blend of raw nuts and seeds is an excellent source of dietary fibre, protein and essential fatty acids such as Omega-3, -6 and -9; as well as essential minerals like calcium, magnesium, potassium, phosphorus, selenium, copper and zinc; and vitamins A, B, D and E. This wonderful nutritional powerhouse has a nutty and sweet taste, and is an easy, quick way to enrich lots of dishes by sprinkling on stir-fries, cereals, yoghurts, smoothies, desserts, fruits and salads.

You can buy LSA in most health food stores or make your own by blending equal parts flaxseeds, sunflower seeds and almonds in the food processor or coffee grinder. Best used fresh but can be stored in an airtight container in the refrigerator for up to 7 days.

3 fresh bananas, peeled (use frozen if you would like a thicker texture to your smoothie)
1 tablespoon hemp protein powder
½ teaspoon ground cinnamon
1 tablespoon flaxseed oil
½ teaspoon raw honey, or to taste
600ml (20fl oz/2½ cups) almond milk
LSA, to sprinkle

Blend all the ingredients together in a blender for 2 minutes. Pour into 2 glasses and sprinkle with a little LSA mix and enjoy.

TURMERIC MYLK (V)

SERVES 2–4

Turmeric is fat-soluble, so be sure to consume it together with some fat – hence the addition of coconut oil here. Black pepper increases the bioavailability of turmeric by over 1,000% – so I've added some of that too.

3 black peppercorns
1 clove
1 cardamom pod
2cm (¾in) piece of fresh ginger
    peeled and cut into thin slices
2cm (¾in) piece of fresh turmeric,
    peeled and cut into thin slices
    (or 1 teaspoon ground turmeric)
1 cinnamon stick
2 dried dates, stoned (pitted)
500ml (17fl oz/2¼ cups) coconut milk
    or almond milk
1 teaspoon melted coconut oil

Place the peppercorns, clove and cardamom pod into a mortar and pestle and slightly crush, then place all the ingredients into a medium saucepan and gently bring to a low simmer. Give an occasional stir. Remove from the heat just before the liquid starts to boil. Cover the saucepan with a lid and allow to infuse for 3–4 hours if possible.

When ready to drink, reheat gently to desired drinking temperature and then strain the liquid through a fine sieve (strainer) before serving. If there is any left, it can be stored, when cold, in the refrigerator for a few days and reheated as required.

GINGER & SPICE MOLASSES FRIANDS

SERVES 12

The combination of warming spices and soft texture of these friands are wonderful. Using molasses as the sweetener with spices, such as cinnamon and clove adds to the rich flavour of these treats. Best eaten warm from the oven, these will last for 3 days in an airtight container.

210g (7½oz/1⅓ cups) dried dates, stoned (pitted)
120ml (4fl oz/½ cup) boiling filtered water
½ teaspoon bicarbonate of soda (baking soda)
120g (4oz/scant 1 cup) buckwheat flour
1 teaspoon gluten-free baking powder
1 teaspoon ground ginger
1 teaspoon ground cinnamon
½ teaspoon ground cloves
100ml (3½fl oz/scant ½ cup) olive oil
2 tablespoons molasses
2 eggs
chopped hazelnuts to decorate

Preheat the oven to 180°C fan/400°F/Gas 6. Lightly grease the 12 sections of a friand tin (pan) with a little coconut oil.

Mix the dates, boiling water and bicarbonate of soda into a small mixing bowl and allow to stand for 10 minutes.

In a separate bowl, whisk together the flour, baking powder and spices. Set aside.

Place the date mixture into a blender, add the olive oil and molasses and blend until smooth. Add the eggs, then the flour mixture and process until just combined.

Pour the mixture into the friand tin and top with chopped hazelnuts. Bake for 20 minutes or until the friands have risen and a skewer comes out clean. Allow the friands to cool in the tin then remove and enjoy!

VIRTUOUS FLAPJACK

MAKES 18 BARS

300g (11oz/3 cups) gluten-free rolled oats
200g (7oz/2 cups) millet flakes
80g (3oz/generous 1¼ cups) coconut flakes
200g (7oz/generous ¾ cup) chopped apricots
40g (1½oz/⅓ cup) goji berries
60g (2oz/½ cup) sunflower seeds
60g (2oz/½ cup) pumpkin seeds
1 tablespoon hemp protein powder
680g (1lb 8oz/scant 2 cups) raw honey
180g (6oz/⅔ cup) tahini paste
2 tablespoons vanilla extract

Preheat the oven to 160°C fan/350°F/ Gas 4. Line a 36 x 20cm (14 x 8in) shallow baking tin (pan) with baking paper (parchment paper). Mix all the dry ingredients, including the fruit and seeds together in a large bowl, using only half the coconut flakes.

Place the honey, tahini and vanilla into a saucepan and heat gently, stirring until melted and runny. Add to the dry mixture and stir thoroughly.

Place the mixture in the tin and spread out evenly. Sprinkle the remaining coconut flakes over and press into the top of the mixture. Bake for 25 minutes or until lightly browned and cooked through.

Allow to cool in the tin, then refrigerate for an hour before cutting into bars.

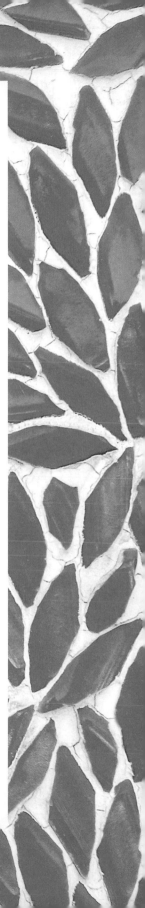

Nurture

This chapter is based on the heart chakra, *anahata*, where we begin to discover our true selves. Since the heart chakra is the midway point, balance becomes an essential principle; both outer balance as well as inner balance are key. Humankind can easily lose its balance between the mind and body in the fast-paced world of today and the Nurture chapter seeks to reunite these elements. The recipes in this chapter are all nutrient-dense and filled with phytonutrients that are truly devoted to healing and restoring, allowing nurture to take place on all levels.

With energy filling our bodies, our will and our determination from the Vitalise third chakra, we now need to push towards transformation. Like plants that push out from their roots in the earth and grow towards the light – we too expand in two directions. While we remain true to our roots, using them to anchor us, we also expand beyond ourselves. In this chakra we learn the art of love and attachment, which connect the forces between the Earth and ourselves. This ultimately creates true balance from within.

KALEOLA

SERVES 6

Buckwheat is a flowering plant that enriches the earth through its cultivation. It's commonly grown where the earth needs to rest and rejuvenate. In the human body it reduces toxic acidic waste and balances the pH level by being alkaline. I use buckwheat in the kitchen when I know I need a lot of energy that day. Since it is a complete protein and has the longest transit time in the gut, buckwheat is both filling and blood sugar stabilising.

Great as a snack, breakfast served with yoghurt or crumbled over a savoury salad this crunchy granola has a reach far beyond the breakfast table.

500g (1lb 2oz) kale
200g (7oz/1 cup) buckwheat groats
125g (4oz/2¼ cups) coconut flakes
150g (5oz/1½ cups) gluten-free rolled oats
100g (3½oz/generous ¾ cup) sunflower seeds
100g (3½oz/generous ¾ cup) flaxseeds
2 tablespoons sesame seeds
120g (4oz/1 cup) cranberries
300g (11oz/scant 1 cup) raw honey
2 tablespoons vanilla extract
50ml (1¾fl oz/scant ¼ cup) olive oil

Preheat the oven to 170°C fan/375°F/ Gas 5. Line 2 or 3 baking trays (baking sheets) with baking paper (parchment paper). Place the kale including the stalks into a food processor and blend until it resembles small crumbs.

Combine the dry ingredients, including the cranberries in a large mixing bowl. Place the honey, vanilla and oil into a saucepan over a low heat until the mixture is runny, which will help to evenly distribute it through the dry ingredients. Remove from the heat.

Pour the warm honey mixture over the dry ingredients and stir thoroughly to combine, then add the kale and coat all the ingredients together. Transfer the granola to the prepared baking trays. It's important not too overcrowd the baking trays. They should only have a 2cm (¾in) thin layer of granola. Bake for 35 minutes or so, until the granola is deep golden brown.

Remove from the oven and allow to cool completely on the baking trays. The granola should be completely dry and not sticky. If it is sticky the granola should be cooked at the same temperature for another 10 minutes, but be careful not to let it burn. (The key to this granola keeping its characteristic clumps is to not touch or move the granola at any stage of its baking or cooling process.)

Once cooled, the granola can be stored in an airtight container. Break up the granola with your fingers as needed.

GREEN BREAKFAST BOWL

SERVES 2

2 eggs
2 tablespoons melted coconut oil
2 garlic cloves, finely chopped
20g (¾oz/scant ¼ cup) raw almonds,
    roughly chopped
20g (¾oz/scant ¼ cup) pumpkin seeds
20g (¾oz/scant ¼ cup) sunflower seeds
100g (3½oz/1 cup) cooked quinoa
¼ teaspoon sea salt
150g (5oz) kale, stalks removed and
    leaves torn into bite-sized pieces
50g (2oz/1 cup) baby spinach leaves
125g (4oz/2¼ cups) halloumi
50g (2oz/1 cup) freshly grated
    coconut flesh
2 lemon wedges
1 avocado, halved, peeled, stoned
    (pitted) and sliced

Put the eggs in a small saucepan with just enough water to cover. Bring to the boil and boil for 3 minutes. Remove the eggs with a slotted spoon, place the eggs under cold running water until cool enough to handle. Very carefully peel off the shells and set aside.

Heat 1 tablespoon of the coconut oil in a large frying pan over a medium heat. Add the garlic and cook, constantly stirring, until the garlic is fragrant and lightly browned. Add the almonds, pumpkin seeds and sunflower seeds and toast until lightly browned. Add the cooked quinoa and the sea salt. Now add the kale and spinach leaves and mix to incorporate. Once the kale and spinach have slightly wilted remove from the heat.

Spoon the mixture into serving bowls then, using the same frying pan, crumble the halloumi into the pan and gently cook until golden on all sides. This will only take a few minutes. Remove from the pan and set aside.

Add the halloumi to each serving bowl. Place the eggs into the frying pan and turn until a little colour is added to each egg. Add an egg to each bowl, followed by the grated coconut flesh, lemon wedges and avocado slices. Serve immediately while still warm.

GREEN DETOX OMELETTE

SERVES 2

Brilliant for those mornings when eggs are needed but an uplifting and light breakfast is actually what you are aiming for. Feel free to use whatever herbs you have in the house and if fresh is not available then dried will do. You can also omit the coconut milk if you prefer.

4 eggs, at room temperature
2 tablespoons coconut milk
2 tablespoons roughly chopped chives
small bunch of parsley, roughly
    chopped
small bunch of coriander (cilantro),
    roughly chopped
2 tablespoons roughly chopped
    dill (dillweed)
2 tablespoons roughly chopped
    chervil
25g (1oz/½ cup) baby spinach,
    roughly chopped
¼ teaspoon fine sea salt
freshly cracked black pepper
2 teaspoons melted coconut oil
lightly dressed salad leaves
    of your choice
2 tablespoons crumbled goat's
    cheese or feta (optional)
1 teaspoon hemp seeds

In a medium mixing bowl, add the eggs and coconut milk and whisk until combined. Add the herbs, spinach and seasoning and whisk again.

Place a large non-stick frying pan over a medium–high heat and add the coconut oil, tilting the pan so that it coats the surface evenly.

Add half of the egg mixture to the pan and quickly swirl the pan around until it forms an even layer over the bottom of the pan. Cook the omelette until the egg is just set, this should take 1–2 minutes. It's done when the edges are dry and the top is no longer runny. Using a spatula, carefully remove the omelette from the pan and place on a large serving plate.

Place half of the lightly dressed salad leaves on top and half the cheese, if using, then sprinkle half the hemp seeds over. Fold the omelette in half and serve with a dash of cracked black pepper.

Repeat with the remaining ingredients to make another filled omelette in the same way.

Pictured L–R (text on pages 104–105): Falafel, Tabouli, Tzatziki, Omega Crackers (text on page 111) and Hummus

MEZZE

Enjoy all of these components together. Picking and mixing is my favourite way to eat these small dishes. This is the perfect example of when the sum is greater than its individual parts (for Omega Crackers see page 111).

FALAFEL

150g (5oz/1 cup) white quinoa, rinsed
225ml (8fl oz/1 cup) filtered water
sea salt
100g (3½oz/1¾ cups) spinach
50g (2oz) parsley
50g (2oz) mint, leaves picked
200g (7oz/1½ cups) frozen peas,
    lightly blanched
2 garlic cloves, chopped
½ teaspoon ground cumin
½ teaspoon ground coriander
½ teaspoon ground sweet paprika
½ teaspoon turmeric
2 eggs
100g (3½oz/generous ⅔ cup)
    buckwheat flour
sesame seeds, to garnish

Preheat the oven to 180°C fan/400°F/ Gas 6. Line 2 baking trays (baking sheets) with baking paper (parchment paper). To cook the quinoa, combine the quinoa, filtered water and a pinch of sea salt in a medium saucepan. Bring to the boil over a medium heat. Once boiling, reduce the heat and allow the quinoa to cook for about 15 minutes uncovered. Watch to check the water level and stir occasionally.

Once all the water has been absorbed and evaporated the quinoa should be cooked. Place a clean tea towel (dishcloth) over the top of the saucepan and replace the lid trying to create a tight seal. This will make the quinoa light and fluffy. Leave to cool for at least 10 minutes.

In the meantime, place the spinach, herbs, peas, garlic, 1 teaspoon sea salt and spices into a food processor and pulse until smooth.

Lightly whisk 2 eggs in a large mixing bowl. Add the quinoa and mix to coat. Add the pea mix from the food processor and mix until thoroughly combined. Mix with a little more or less of the buckwheat flour to bind and form a soft but not sticky mixture. Taste for seasoning.

Using your hands, roll into walnut-sized balls and place onto the prepared baking trays. If you are short of time, you can always use an ice-cream scoop instead of your hands to portion the falafel onto the baking trays. Sprinkle the falafel with sesame seeds.

Bake for 15 minutes or until the falafel feel firm but not hard. Remove from the oven and either enjoy warm or allow to cool before serving.

HUMMUS (V)

2 x 400g cans (14oz) chickpeas,
    drained, reserving 3 tablespoons
    of liquid
juice of 1 lemon
1 tablespoon tahini paste
30g (1oz) fresh coriander (cilantro)
    leaves, washed
2 garlic cloves
2 teaspoons ground cumin
3 tablespoons olive oil
2 teaspoons sea salt
cracked black pepper, to taste

Place all the ingredients into a food processor and blend until smooth, stopping and scraping down the sides as necessary. Adjust the seasoning to taste and transfer to a serving bowl.

TZATZIKI

½ cucumber, washed and grated
2 pinches of sea salt
250g (9oz/1 cup) full-fat Greek yoghurt
juice of ½ lemon
6 mint leaves, finely chopped
freshly cracked black pepper

Place the grated cucumber into a fine sieve (strainer), set over a medium bowl. Sprinkle the sea salt over the cucumber, toss gently and allow to stand for 30 minutes.

In a separate medium mixing bowl, add the Greek yoghurt, lemon juice and mint and stir well. Squeeze the remaining liquid from the cucumber and add to the mixture. Stir to incorporate again, then season with the pepper. Taste and add a little more salt if necessary. You may like to add a little more lemon juice or mint too. Transfer to a serving bowl and chill until ready to serve.

TABOULI

1 cucumber, peeled and cut into
    5mm (¼in) dice
5 tomatoes, washed and cut into
    5mm (¼in) dice
½ red onion, very finely diced
large bunch of flat-leaf parsley, leaves
    finely chopped
small bunch of mint, leaves finely
    chopped
small bunch of coriander (cilantro),
    finely chopped
juice of 1 lemon
1 tablespoon pomegranate molasses
4 tablespoons extra-virgin olive oil
¼ teaspoon sea salt

Combine all the ingredients together in a medium mixing bowl. Adjust the seasoning to taste, transfer to a serving bowl and set aside.

SPRING GREENS & MUNG BEAN SALAD (V)

SERVES 4

Add as many green vegetables as you can fit into one serving! Mung beans have the most wonderful, delicate crisp crunch, as well as being packed with protein, vitamins, minerals and antioxidants, making them the perfect addition to this – and other – salads.

140g (4½oz/¾ cup) dried green
    mung beans
sea salt
100g (3½oz/⅔ cup) fresh, shelled or
    frozen peas, quickly blanched
100g (3½oz/⅔ cup) fresh, shelled or
    frozen edamame beans, quickly
    blanched
125g (4oz) sugar snap peas, washed
    and quickly blanched
3 spring onions (scallions), trimmed
    and thinly sliced on a harsh angle
200g (7oz) asparagus spears, trimmed
100g (3½oz) French beans, trimmed
6 radishes, washed and cut in half
    lengthways
2 broccoli stems, trimmed and then
    peeled
20g (¾oz) flat-leaf parsley leaves,
    washed and roughly chopped
30g (1oz/½ cup) pea shoots, washed

For the dressing
100g (3½oz/generous ⅓ cup)
    tahini paste
2 small garlic cloves, peeled and
    crushed
1 tablespoon tamari soy sauce
1 tablespoon pure maple syrup
2 tablespoons cider (apple cider)
    vinegar
pinch of sea salt
2–3 tablespoons filtered water

Begin by soaking the mung beans in water overnight. Make sure to cover the beans with at least 2cm (¾in) filtered water above the beans and add a pinch of salt. Cover with a cloth and in the morning the beans should have soaked up the water and turned nice and plump. They should be crisp to eat and have slightly cracked in appearance. If not then change the water and continue to soak for a further 2 hours.

Drain the beans through a colander and remove any beans which have not softened during the soaking process.

Whisk together all the ingredients for the dressing in a small mixing bowl. Add enough filtered water to reach a desired honey-like consistency, then pour the dressing over the mung beans and allow to soak again.

Combine all the remaining salad ingredients, except the broccoli stems, parsley and pea shoots, in a large bowl. Using a vegetable peeler, shave the broccoli stems over the top of the salad. Add the dressed mung beans and mix together using your hands. Make sure the dressing coats all the vegetables. Place the salad onto a large serving platter and serve scattered with parsley leaves and pea shoots.

STUFFED COURGETTE FLOWERS WITH CORN & PEACH SALSA (V)

SERVES 3

This delicious and innovative recipe is best served straight from the oven while still piping hot. To skin peaches, make a small cross cut in the base of each. Place in a bowl, cover with boiling water, leave for 30 seconds, then drain and pull off the skins.

9 courgette (zucchini) flowers
1 tablespoon extra virgin olive oil
sea salt flakes
150g (5oz/1½ cups) pink quinoa (see page 108)
salad greens, for serving

For the stuffing
90g (3¼oz/⅔ cup) Brazil nuts, soaked in hot filtered water
1 garlic clove, roughly chopped
1½ teaspoons Dijon mustard
1 tablespoon cider (apple cider) vinegar
1 tablespoon roughly chopped tarragon leaves
1 tablespoon roughly chopped chives
1 sprig of lemon thyme, leaves
finely grated zest and juice of 1 lemon
¼ teaspoon sea salt
freshly cracked black pepper

For the corn & peach salsa
3 yellow peaches, skinned and diced into cubes
1 corn on the cob, chargrilled and kernels removed
½ small red chilli, seeded and finely chopped
finely grated zest of 1 lime
2cm (¾in) piece of ginger, peeled and finely grated
1 tablespoon finely chopped mint
1 tablespoon finely chopped coriander (cilantro)

Preheat the oven to 200°C fan/430°F/Gas 7 and line a flat baking tray (baking sheet) with baking paper (parchment paper). Rinse the courgette flowers under cold running water, shake gently and then leave on kitchen paper (paper towels) to dry. Using a small paring knife, make a slit on one side of each flower. Cut the yellow furry stamen from the inside of the flower and discard.

Place all the stuffing ingredients in a food processor and blend until smooth, stopping and scraping down the sides as necessary. Taste for seasoning and adjust accordingly. Transfer the contents to a small bowl and cover with clingfilm (plastic wrap). Chill in the refrigerator for 1 hour.

Make the grilled corn and peach salsa by combining all the ingredients together in a small bowl, seasoning to taste. Set aside.

To stuff the flowers, place 2 teaspoons of the stuffing mixture into each flower. It is easiest if you fill them through the slit on the side of each flower. Use your hands to press the mixture into the flower and twist the ends closed.

Place each flower on the prepared baking sheet. Using a pastry brush, lightly coat each flower completely with olive oil and sprinkle with a little sea salt. Bake in the oven for 15 minutes until they turn crispy and golden brown.

To serve, place some of the salad leaves onto 3 serving plates, sprinkle some pink quinoa over the plate and a spoonful of the salsa, then place 3 hot stuffed courgette flowers onto each plate and serve immediately.

CLEMENTINE, CUCUMBER & AVOCADO CEVICHE WITH PINK QUINOA (V)

SERVES 4

For the pink quinoa

100g (3½oz/½ cup) white quinoa
200ml (7fl oz/scant 1 cup) filtered water
pinch of sea salt flakes
60ml (2fl oz/¼ cup) beetroot (beet) juice

For the ceviche

1 cucumber, peeled and cut into 1cm (½in) dice
2 green guindilla/florina peppers, seeded and cut into 1cm (½in) dice
3 clementines, peeled and segmented
finely grated zest and juice of 2 limes
2 tablespoons finely chopped coriander (cilantro)
2 tablespoons finely chopped mint leaves
sea salt and freshly cracked black pepper
flesh of 2 avocados, mashed
toasted coconut chips, to serve

Combine the quinoa, filtered water and a pinch of sea salt in a medium saucepan. Bring to the boil over a medium heat, once simmering, reduce the heat and allow the quinoa to cook for about 15 minutes uncovered. Watch to check the water level and stir occasionally. Once all the water has been absorbed the quinoa should be cooked. Place a clean tea towel (dishcloth) over the top of the saucepan and replace the lid trying to create a tight seal. This will make the quinoa light and fluffy. Leave to cool for at least 10 minutes.

Remove the lid and tea towel from the saucepan and, using a fork, fluff up the quinoa. Pour the beetroot juice into the quinoa and, using the same fork, stir to coat the quinoa in the juice. Once the desired pink colour has been reached, set aside.

Place the cucumber and green pepper pieces into a medium mixing bowl. Slice each individual piece of clementine in half lengthways and add to the bowl. Add the rest of the ingredients and season to taste.

To serve, place a food ring on each of your plates and, using a spoon, firmly pack the ceviche mix into the mould. Once the mould is filled, remove the ring, then sprinkle some of the pink quinoa and coconut chips across each plate.

RAW ASPARAGUS MOUSSE (V)

SERVES 4

350g (12oz) fresh asparagus spears, cut in short lengths, woody ends discarded
200g (7oz/1¼ cups) fresh shelled or frozen peas
½ cauliflower, cut into florets, stump and leaves removed
½ small red onion
flesh of 4 avocados
juice of 2 limes
large bunch of coriander (cilantro)
large bunch of basil
60ml (2fl oz/¼ cup) olive oil
1 teaspoon mustard seeds
½ teaspoon sea salt and freshly cracked black pepper
120g (4oz/1¼ cups) raw pecans, roughly chopped
Omega Crackers (see page opposite)
1 tablespoon hemp seeds

Place the asparagus sprigs and peas into a food processor and blend until smooth. Now add the cauliflower florets and onion, mix again until all the ingredients become incorporated. Add the avocado flesh, lime juice, herbs, olive oil, mustard seeds and seasoning and blend until the mixture resembles a soft mousse.

Remove from the food processor, add the chopped pecans and mix to incorporate. Taste for seasoning and adjust accordingly.

To serve, take a serving plate and, using an ice-cream scoop, place 2 scoops of the mousse on the plate, then add the Omega Crackers and hemp seeds. Repeat for all other plates and serve immediately.

OMEGA CRACKERS (V)

SERVES 8
(PICTURED ON PAGE 103)

50g (2oz/½ cup) sunflower seeds
50g (2oz/½ cup) pumpkin seeds, plus
    extra to garnish
200g (7oz/1½ cups) buckwheat flour
200g (7oz/2 cups) quinoa flakes
2 teaspoons poppy seeds
150g (5oz/1 cup) flaxseeds
150g (5oz/1 cup) sesame seeds
2 teaspoons fine sea salt
1 teaspoon ground turmeric
1 teaspoon ground coriander
1 teaspoon ground cumin
2 teaspoons sweet paprika
2 teaspoons fennel seeds
500ml (17fl oz/2¼ cups) filtered water
sea salt flakes

Preheat the oven to 170°C fan/375°F/ Gas 5. Line 4 flat baking trays (baking sheets) with baking paper (parchment paper).

Mix all the dry ingredients together in a large mixing bowl and stir to combine. Using your hands, make a well in the middle of the mixture and pour in the water. Start to combine the mixture to create a paste. Once incorporated start to spread the mixture onto the prepared baking trays using clean, wet hands. The mixture should be no thicker than 2–3mm (⅛in). It should be as thin as you can spread it out on the trays. Add water if you need to help spread the paste out.

Once evenly spread onto the baking trays, sprinkle with a few extra pumpkin seeds and the sea salt flakes. Score with a knife into desired sizes and shapes, then bake in the oven for 45 minutes. The trick to these crackers is to make sure you open the oven door every 10 minutes for 10 seconds to allow the moisture to evaporate from the oven. The crackers should start to lift away from the sides of the baking trays once cooked. Depending on how thinly you spread the paste out onto the trays, your crackers may need a little more time to cook through (particularly those towards the centres of the trays).

Once cooked through, remove from the oven and allow to cool completely on the trays before cutting or breaking into crackers. Store in an airtight container.

GREEN QUINOA BURGERS

SERVES 20

Crispy on the outside and soft on the inside, these burgers are so versatile as a snack or lunchtime protein side.

1 butternut squash, peeled and cut into small 1cm (½in) cubes
3 tablespoons melted coconut oil
1 teaspoon ground cumin
1 teaspoon ground coriander
1 teaspoon sea salt flakes
350g (12oz/3 cups) cooked quinoa
200g (7oz) chard leaves, lightly steamed
2 spring onions (scallions), finely sliced
135g (4½oz/scant 1 cup) crumbled goat's cheese
small bunch of parsley, finely chopped
2 eggs, lightly whisked
1 teaspoon sea salt
freshly cracked black pepper
45g (1½oz/¼ cup) rice flour
1 teaspoon sesame seeds

For the dressing
3 tablespoons probiotic yoghurt
juice of ½ lemon
1 dill sprig, roughly chopped

Preheat the oven to 180°C fan/400°F/Gas 6. Place the squash on a baking tray (baking sheet). Drizzle with 1 tablespoon of the coconut oil and sprinkle over the cumin and coriander. Using your hands, toss the squash to coat in the oil and spices, then sprinkle with the sea salt flakes. Roast in the oven for 15 minutes or until soft and cooked through.

Combine the cooked squash pieces, cooked quinoa, steamed chard leaves, spring onion, goat's cheese, parsley, eggs and a little salt and pepper and gently toss together. Add the rice flour, just enough so that the mix comes together. Cover and leave to cool, then chill in the refrigerator for at least 30 minutes.

Once the mixture is chilled, take a small handful sized piece into your hands and form into a small patty shape. Repeat with the remaining mixture, then sprinkle a few sesame seeds over the patties.

Place a large frying pan over a medium–high heat and add 1 tablespoon of the coconut oil. Tilt to coat the pan in the oil and then add the patties in batches and fry for 3–4 minutes on either side until browned. Add the remaining tablespoon of coconut oil when needed and repeat until all the patties are cooked.

Place the patties onto a baking tray and bake in the oven for 5–7 minutes or just enough time to cook through. Remove from the oven. Mix all the ingredients for the dressing together in a bowl and serve drizzled on top of the burgers.

NURTURE SMOOTHIE (V)

SERVES 2

flesh of 1 ripe avocado
3 sprigs of mint
1 tablespoon flaxseed oil
1 teaspoon moringa powder
½ lime, peeled and pith removed
500ml (17fl oz/2¼ cups) coconut water

Place all the ingredients into a blender and blend for 2 minutes. Pour into 2 glasses and serve.

GREEN GODDESS JUICE (V)

SERVES 2

50g (2oz/1 cup) spinach leaves
½ lemon, peeled and pith removed
2.5cm (1in) piece of fresh ginger, peeled
3 celery sticks
1 large fennel bulb
1 cucumber

Pass all the ingredients through a juicer and serve immediately.

Pictured L–R: Nurture Smoothie, Green Goddess Juice and Green Dream Juice

GREEN DREAM JUICE (V)

SERVES 2

This juice isn't for the light-hearted. I designed this juice to pack a punch and kick-start your day. Easily available from health food stores, the addition of *Ginkgo biloba* although optional will improve the circulation to your brain, help combat poor concentration, confusion, fatigue, headaches, dizziness, depression and anxiety. So don't reach for the coffee if you're struggling to switch on, get yourself a juice and add some gingko drops pronto.

50g (2oz/1 cup) spinach leaves
5mm (¼in) piece of fresh horseradish, peeled
3 celery sticks
1 cucumber
3 apples
12 drops of Ginkgo biloba extract

Pass all the ingredients, except the ginkgo drops, through a juicer. Add the drops and give a gentle stir. Serve in two glasses.

LEMON VERBENA BLISS BALLS

(V) MAKES 20

250g (9oz/1½ cups) raw macadamia
    nuts or cashews
20 lemon verbena leaves or 2
    lemon verbena tea bags
filtered hot water to soak
115g (4oz/1¼ cups) desiccated
    (dry unsweetened) coconut plus
    2 tablespoons extra for coating
1 teaspoon finely grated lemon zest
juice of 1 lemon
60ml (2fl oz/¼ cup) light coconut
    nectar
2 tablespoons melted coconut oil
1 teaspoon vanilla extract
pinch of Himalayan sea salt

Place the macadamia nuts and lemon verbena leaves or tea bags into a medium bowl. Pour enough of the hot filtered water to cover and allow to soak for 2 hours. Remove the lemon verbena from the bowl and drain the macadamia nuts through a colander.

Place all the ingredients into a food processor and blend until a smooth dough forms, stopping and scraping down the sides as necessary. Remove from the food processor and place into a medium bowl. Leave to cool, then chill in the refrigerator for 1 hour.

Once chilled, roll a walnut-sized portion of the mixture in the palm of your hand. Place the ball into a plastic lock seal bag with the 2 extra tablespoons of desiccated coconut, then roll the remaining mixture into balls. Place in the bag, then shake until the balls are coated with coconut. Store in the bag or an airtight container in the refrigerator for up to 2 weeks.

Strengthen

This chapter is based on the fifth chakra, *vissudha* which means purification. This detoxification process needs to take place in order to rid our bodies of the toxins within it. This purifying system focuses on strengthening two areas within our bodies; the throat and the thyroid.

The throat is the narrowest passage within the whole chakra system and it is a bottleneck for our energy systems to flow freely. It also acts as a filter system, sorting through messages from the body and connecting them with information in the brain. We can release and free up this passage by eating and cooking soothing foods for our throats such as warming soups, restorative tea and moist fruits.

The thyroid is the other major organ in this chakra, it is responsible for determining our growth and developing tissues for our body, but most importantly, in adult life the thyroid regulates our temperature and our metabolism. Foods rich in iodine, such as sea plants, feature in this chapter because the cells in the thyroid are the only ones that can absorb iodine.

The fifth chakra is where our individual creative expression is at its highest. This self-expression becomes the means for relaying to the outer world what is really inside us.

CRANBERRY & ORANGE BREAKFAST MUFFINS

MAKES 12

These flourless muffins are packed full of protein from the use of ground almonds. They are a great breakfast if you are trying to avoid sugar as these muffins only use the sweetness of banana and dried cranberries. Make sure you use overly ripe bananas so the mixture has a soft consistency and a sweet flavour.

400g (14oz/4 cups) ground almonds
4 teaspoons baking powder
2 teaspoons ground cinnamon
8 eggs, whisked
2 teaspoons vanilla extract
finely grated zest of 1 orange
450g (1lb/scant 2 cups) mashed
    overripe banana
200g (7oz/1⅔ cups) dried cranberries
350g (12oz) carrots, finely grated in
    food processor
1 tablespoon pumpkin seeds,
    to garnish

Preheat the oven to 180°C fan/400°F/ Gas 6. Line a muffin tin (pan) with paper cases. In a large bowl, combine all the ingredients and thoroughly stir together, making sure all the ingredients are incorporated.

Transfer the batter to the muffin cases and sprinkle each with pumpkin seeds. Bake for 30 minutes or until cooked through and the centres spring back when lightly pressed. Remove from the oven and allow to cool.

ELDERBERRY & ECHINACEA GUMMIES (V)

MAKES 20

Take these delicious little jellies daily to avoid colds and flu or take every few hours to help beat the symptoms faster. If you use a different vegetarian gelatine, make up according to the packet instructions for the amount of liquid in the recipe.

1 tablespoon melted coconut oil
350ml (12fl oz/1½ cups) elderberry
    syrup (or blackcurrant syrup)
1 sachet Vege-Gel (or other vegetarian
    gelatine)
225ml (8fl oz/1 cup) hot filtered water
2 tablespoons echinacea extract

Begin by greasing a tray of candy or chocolate moulds (molds) or a glass tray with the coconut oil to prevent the gummies from sticking. In a medium jug (pitcher), add half the elderberry syrup with the Vege-Gel powder and quickly whisk together to dissolve the powder. Add the hot water and stir quickly until smooth. Now add the rest of the elderberry syrup and the echinacea and stir or whisk until completely smooth.

Pour into the moulds or tray and place in the refrigerator for 2 hours or until completely firm. Pop out of the moulds or cut the set jelly on the tray into small lozenges and store in an airtight container with baking paper (parchment paper) between layers for up to a week.

THE HERBAL CAULDRON (V)

SERVES 4

2cm (¾in) piece of fresh turmeric,
    peeled and thinly sliced
      (or 1 teaspoon ground turmeric)
2cm (¾in) piece of fresh ginger,
    peeled and thinly sliced
1 garlic clove
1 bay leaf
pinch of ground cinnamon
3 black peppercorns
2 whole cardamom pods
500ml (17fl oz/2¼ cups)
    vegetable stock

Place all the ingredients together in a medium saucepan and bring to a low simmer for about 20 minutes. Remove from the heat and strain through a fine sieve (strainer). Serve the broth while still hot.

GINGER, SAGE & MANUKA THROAT DROPS

MAKES 8 DROPS

These throat drops are particularly good for a dry, irritated cough. Where the throat has become sore and inflamed slippery elm is used to protect the mucous membranes of the body and help soothe the pain associated with a dry cough. Take throughout the day when a sore throat or cough are particularly troubling.

1 lemon, peeled
5cm (2in) piece of fresh ginger
10 sage leaves, washed
2 tablespoons manuka honey
25g (1oz/¼ cup) slippery elm powder, plus extra for coating

Line a baking tray (baking sheet) with baking paper (parchment paper). Pass the lemon, ginger and sage leaves through a juicer. Place the combined juice into a small bowl along with the manuka honey and stir to combine. Add the slippery elm powder and stir until a smooth paste is formed.

Using your hands, roll the paste into small balls about the size of a marble. Roll the balls in a little more slippery elm powder, then place a thumb print in the middle of each ball to create a little indent. Place the drops onto the prepared baking tray and allow to dry for 2 days in a warm, dry place. Store the drops in a glass jar for up to 3 months.

GRILLED WATERMELON & GOAT'S CHEESE SALAD

SERVES 2

The smoky flavour of the grilled watermelon with the goat's cheese and fresh salsa verde creates an interesting depth to this dish that cuts straight through the sweetness of the watermelon.

For the salsa verde
handful of flat-leaf parsley leaves
handful of mint leaves
handful of coriander (cilantro) leaves
juice of 2 lemons
freshly ground black pepper
100ml (3½fl oz/scant ½ cup) extra-virgin olive oil
½ teaspoon sea salt

For the salad
2 tablespoons melted coconut oil
4 watermelon slices
2 slices of round goat's cheese
finely chopped raw pistachio crumbs and small handful of basil leaves, to garnish

To make the salsa verde, process all the ingredients in a food processor until a liquid paste has developed. Keep adding olive oil until a thick pouring consistency is achieved. Season to taste and set aside.

Place a griddle pan with the coconut oil over a medium–high heat and, when hot, sear the watermelon slices on both sides until striped dark brown. Remove from the heat and set aside.

Arrange the watermelon slices and goat's cheese on 2 serving plates. Drizzle a little salsa verde over the goat's cheese, then sprinkle with the pistachio crumbs and add the basil leaves. Serve immediately.

SOBA NOODLE BUDDHA BOWL (V)

SERVES 4

A buddha bowl has become a very popular yoga meal. Typically they are meal-sized bowls filled with simple, pure food. To create your own buddha bowl, find a unique bowl which you can use as a symbol for your nourishment and gratitude. A buddha bowl is supposed to excite your mind with its rainbow coloured ingredients which are full of energy. Enjoy the creation of this dish and be mindful of how nourishing it is for your body.

For the broth
1.2 litres (40fl oz/5 cups) mushroom stock
1 star anise
2 cardamom pods
1 tablespoon peeled and julienned fresh ginger
100g (3½oz) soba noodles
250g (9oz/2¾ cups) fresh chestnut (cremini) and enoki mushrooms (or mushrooms of your choice)

For the bowl
75g (2½oz/1 cup) finely shredded red cabbage leaves
150g (5oz/1 cup) peeled carrots
75g (2½oz/1 cup) finely shredded Savoy cabbage
75g (2½oz) sugar snap peas
90g (3oz/1 cup) bean sprouts, washed
juice of 1 lime
fresh coriander (cilantro) leaves
1 fresh chilli, cut into thin slices (optional)
mixed sesame seeds
lime wedges
tamari soy sauce, to taste

Place all the ingredients for the broth, except the noodles and mushrooms, into a large saucepan and bring to the boil. Once boiling reduce the heat to a gentle simmer, add the buckwheat noodles and mushrooms and cook for 5 minutes or until the noodles are cooked through.

Divide the mixture among 4 serving bowls, discarding the cardamom pods and star anise if you prefer. Begin to add the vegetables into the broth by piling a little of each type around the outside of the bowl. Add a squeeze of lime to each bowl, followed by soy, the fresh coriander leaves, chilli (if using), a sprinkling of sesame seeds and a lime wedge. Serve immediately with chopsticks, a spoon to drink the broth at the end and add tamari to taste.

STRAWBERRY & SPINACH SALAD

SERVES 2–4

I came across this salad when I was travelling through Alaska. I was staying in a small copper mining town, which was run on a single generator. We were so far from civilisation; this was the last thing I expected to find. The strawberries create a lovely thick dressing which coats the spinach and chard leaves thickly and decadently.

For the dressing
150g (5oz/1 cup) strawberries, trimmed and halved
2 tablespoons balsamic vinegar
1 tablespoon red wine vinegar
1 tablespoon lemon juice
1 garlic clove, chopped
¼ teaspoon Dijon mustard

For the salad
250g (9oz) asparagus spears, trimmed
1 tablespoon melted coconut oil
50g (2oz/1 cup) baby spinach leaves
50g (2oz/1 cup) baby chard leaves
100g (3½oz/generous ½ cup) crumbled goat's cheese
80g (3oz/generous ½ cup) toasted hazelnuts (filberts), roughly chopped

For the dressing, place all the ingredients into a blender and blend until smooth. Remove from the blender and set aside.

Place a griddle pan over a high heat. Toss the asparagus in the oil, then place on griddle pan and cook until tender and charred, about 2 minutes each side. Remove from the pan and cut into long slender strips. Set aside.

Combine the spinach and chard leaves in a large mixing bowl. Pour the strawberry dressing over the leaves and toss to combine. Add the asparagus strips, crumbled goat's cheese and roughly chopped hazelnuts and serve immediately.

SAVOURY PEAR & FENNEL SALAD (V)

SERVES 4

The dressing for this salad is one you may not have seen before, but the sweetness of the carrot juice works perfectly with the cleansing nip of the ginger and the sweet linger of balsamic.

For the roasted pears
2 pears, cut into quarters, cores removed
sea salt and freshly cracked black pepper

For the chestnut purée
100g (3½oz/generous ¾ cup) cooked chestnuts
75ml (2½fl oz/scant ⅓ cup) filtered water
1 tablespoon vanilla extract

For the dressing
2 carrots
2cm (¾in) piece of fresh ginger
2 tablespoons balsamic vinegar

For the salad
1 teaspoon melted coconut oil
2 fennel bulbs, cut into 5mm (¼in) slices lengthways
6 radishes, halved lengthways
100g (3½oz/generous 2 cups) lamb's lettuce leaves
50g (2oz/generous ⅓ cup) roasted hazelnuts (filberts), roughly chopped

Preheat the oven to 200°C fan/430°F/ Gas 7. Line a baking tray (baking sheet) with baking paper (parchment paper). Place the pear quarters on the prepared baking tray, and sprinkle them with sea salt and freshly cracked black pepper. Roast in the oven for 20–30 minutes until the pears are golden and juicy.

Meanwhile, make the chestnut purée. Place the cooked chestnuts in a high-speed blender or food processor with the filtered water and vanilla extract and process until smooth. You may need to add a little more water to help it, but only add a teaspoon at a time. Set aside.

To make the dressing, pass the carrots and ginger through a juicer. Collect the juice, then add the balsamic vinegar. Whisk to combine, then season with a little sea salt and freshly cracked black pepper.

For the fennel, place a griddle pan over a high heat and brush the griddle with a little coconut oil. Add the fennel slices and cook for 1 minute either side. Remove from the pan and set aside.

To assemble the plates, place a spoonful of the chestnut purée onto each plate. Place a few fennel slices in the middle and then 2 pear quarters on top of the fennel slices. Place radish halves and a few lamb's lettuce leaves around the plate, then drizzle the dressing over the plate and sprinkle with the roasted hazelnuts. Serve immediately.

FIG & HALLOUMI SALAD

SERVES 4

For the dressing

50g (2oz/⅓ cup) pine nuts (pine kernels), soaked in filtered water for 2 hours
1 small shallot, roughly chopped
2 tablespoons apple cider vinegar
2½ tablespoons extra-virgin olive oil
½ teaspoon Himalayan salt
½ teaspoon sumac, plus extra to garnish
2 tablespoons filtered water

For the salad

250g (9oz) halloumi
1 teaspoon melted coconut oil
200g (7oz/4 cups) mixture of rocket (arugula) and kale (or salad leaves of your choice)
4 figs, torn or cut into quarters
2 tablespoons pomegranate seeds

First make the dressing. Drain the pine nuts and place them in a blender or food processor. Add the shallot, vinegar, olive oil, salt and sumac, and with the motor running, pour the water through the spout, a splash at a time, to achieve the desired consistency. Set aside.

Cut the halloumi into 5mm (¼in) thick slices. Heat a medium non-stick frying pan over a high heat, add the coconut oil and sear the halloumi on both sides, until just golden. Tear the slices of halloumi up with your hands into bite-sized pieces, then arrange salad leaves, figs and halloumi on serving plates. Drizzle with the salad dressing and scatter the pomegranate seed over the top. Dust with a little more sumac and serve immediately.

BEETROOT RAVIOLI WITH KALE & SEAWEED SALAD (V)

SERVES 4

My kitchen is my sanctuary, where I express myself and feel connected to my soul. Yoga also offers me this experience, so whether I am on the mat or in my kitchen, the connection I experience renews me, offering clarity and perspective.

Food is never too far from my thoughts; this salad came from a creative moment while on a yoga retreat. I was thinking about wanting to use seaweed in my cooking. Seaweed is high in iodine and consuming healthy levels of iodine is important for maintaining a healthy thyroid (a gland in your neck which helps produce and regulate hormones and metabolism).

For the mushroom ravioli

100g (3½oz) chestnut (cremini) mushrooms
120g (4oz/generous ¾ cup) raw cashew, soaked for 2 hours in filtered water
pinch of sea salt

For the kale & seaweed salad

15g (½oz/¼ cup) dried arame, wakame or other strands of dried seaweed (such as hijiki)
filtered water to soak the seaweed
200g (7oz) kale, stalks removed and leaves roughly chopped
5cm (2in) piece of fresh ginger, peeled and cut into thin matchsticks
2 tablespoons sesame seeds, toasted
1 tablespoon hemp seeds
75g (2½oz/½ cup) raw pistachios, chopped
60ml (2fl oz/¼ cup) tamari soy sauce
2 tablespoons toasted sesame oil
2 large rainbow beetroot (beet) or white radish, trimmed and peeled
3 tablespoons raw pistachios, roughly chopped

First, make the filling. Place the mushrooms, soaked cashews and salt into a food processor and blend until smooth. Set aside.

Place the dried arame seaweed and enough boiling filtered water to cover and allow to soak for 20 minutes until soft. Drain the seaweed, reserving 20ml (¾fl oz/4 teaspoons) of the soaking water and place the drained seaweed into a large mixing bowl.

Meanwhile, place the kale in a large frying pan with a few tablespoons of filtered water and sauté until the kale just begins to wilt. Drain the kale and rinse under cold water to refresh. Place the kale in a salad spinner or in a clean tea towel (dishcloth) and pat dry. Add the kale to the large mixing bowl with the seaweed and sprinkle with the ginger, sesame seeds, hemp seeds and pistachios.

Place the tamari, reserved soaking water and sesame oil in a jug (pitcher): and whisk to combine, then pour over the salad and toss together.

Using a mandolin, cut the rainbow beetroot or white radish into very thin slices; you will need 16 full slices. Cut a crescent shape out of 8 of the slices.

Place 2 full round slices on each of the serving plates, then place a dollop of the mushroom ravioli filling onto each slice. Place a crescent piece of the rainbow beetroot on top of the filling to create the ravioli.

Place a portion of the seaweed salad on the plates and sprinkle with a few chopped pistachios before serving.

QUINOA-STUFFED COURGETTES WITH PICKLED FENNEL & ASPARAGUS

SERVES 6

Available in the late summer and autumn months these perfectly spherical courgettes (zucchini) are native to Italy. Their gorgeous shape, makes them perfect for stuffing and this creamy quinoa and olive filling only adds to the decadent theme. If round courgettes aren't available you can use a yellow squash instead or other squash varieties.

For the pickled fennel & asparagus
1 fennel bulb
2 asparagus spears, diagonally sliced very thinly
1 tablespoon fresh dill (dillweed), chopped
juice of ½ lemon
1 tablespoon cider (apple cider) vinegar
2 tablespoons extra-virgin olive oil
sea salt and freshly cracked black pepper

For the cauliflower purée
4 teaspoons coconut oil
1 leek, roughly chopped
1 cauliflower, curds only, separated into small florets
200ml (7fl oz/scant 1 cup) rice milk
1 vegetable stock cube
sea salt and freshly cracked black pepper
a little freshly grated nutmeg

For the quinoa stuffed round courgettes (zucchini)
125g (4oz/1¼ cups) white quinoa
250ml (9fl oz/generous 1 cup) vegetable stock
6 round courgettes (zucchini)
4 garlic cloves, finely chopped
1 brown onion, finely chopped
50g (2oz/⅓ cup) soft goat's cheese
1 tablespoon thyme leaves
handful of pitted black olives
sea salt and freshly cracked black pepper
1 tablespoon extra-virgin olive oil

For the miso & caper drizzle
1 teaspoon miso paste
50ml (2fl oz/¼ cup) extra-virgin olive oil
2 teaspoons capers

For the pickled fennel and asparagus, trim the fennel and cut in half. Using a vegetable peeler or mandolin, slice very thinly. Place in a bowl along with the asparagus slices and chopped dill, then add the lemon juice, vinegar and olive oil. Toss together and add sea salt and freshly cracked black pepper as needed. Set aside.

For the cauliflower purée, heat the coconut oil in a medium heavy-based saucepan. Add the leek and sauté until soft but not browned. Add the cauliflower, stirring to coat in the softened leeks and cook for a few minutes before adding the rice milk and stock cube. Reduce the heat, cover and simmer for 15 minutes. Once the cauliflower is completely cooked, remove from the heat and allow to cool slightly. Use a hand-held blender to purée until smooth. Season with salt, pepper and a little nutmeg. Set aside and keep warm.

Rinse the quinoa in a colander and drain well. Bring the vegetable stock to the boil in a medium saucepan. Add the quinoa, stir, cover, reduce the heat and cook for about 15 minutes until the quinoa is light and fluffy.

To prepare the courgettes, cut a very thin slice from the bottom of each courgette, so that they can stand alone. Cut a 2cm (¾in) lid from the top of each, making sure to keep the lids. Using a small teaspoon, scoop out the inner courgette flesh from each round courgette, being careful to remove as much as possible without piercing the skins. Place the flesh onto a large chopping (cutting) board and dice into small pieces. Place the empty courgettes with their lids into a large baking tin (pan).

Preheat the oven to 200°C fan/430°F/ Gas 7. Using a large non-stick frying pan, add the garlic and onion and sauté over a medium–low heat until translucent. Add the courgette flesh and cook over a medium heat, stirring to cook the courgettes evenly. Add the cooked quinoa and remove from the heat. Add the goat's cheese and fold through, allowing the cheese to melt. Add the fresh thyme and black olives and stir to completely combine. Season to taste. Spoon this mixture into the empty round courgettes and replace the courgette lids. Pour about 1cm (½in) water into the baking tin. Sprinkle with salt and pepper, drizzle with olive oil and cover with foil. Bake for 45–60 minutes until just tender. Remove the foil and return to the oven for another 20 minutes until lightly browned.

Meanwhile, make the miso and caper drizzle. Place the miso paste and olive oil in a small saucepan and whisk to incorporate, then add the capers and stir through. Heat through but do not boil.

To serve, place a dollop of cauliflower purée in the centre of each serving plate. Place a stuffed courgette, lid removed, on top of the purée, then add a spoonful of pickled fennel salad on top of the courgette. Drizzle a little miso and caper oil around the plates and serve immediately.

HOT PENICILLIN

SERVES 1

When a cold has taken hold, there is no better 'cure all' than this hot penicillin. Sweet and soothing the healing properties of this tea are second to none. Drunk throughout the day while convalescing this herbal concoction will have you back on your feet in no time. If elderberry is unavailable, add a tablespoon of blackcurrants to the saucepan instead.

1 garlic clove, finely chopped
2cm (¾in) piece of fresh ginger, peeled and thinly sliced
juice and flesh of 1 lemon
2 tablespoons manuka honey
1 tablespoon elderberry syrup
250ml (9fl oz/generous 1 cup) filtered water
15 drops of echinacea extract

Place all the ingredients, except the echinacea drops, into a saucepan. Slowly bring to the boil, while stirring to dissolve the manuka honey. Once boiling remove from the heat and strain through a fine sieve (strainer). Add the echinacea drops and serve in a comforting mug.

APRICOT & SAGE SPRITZERS (V)

SERVES 4

4 large sage leaves
6 ripe apricots, stoned (pitted)
3 tablespoons filtered water
2 tablespoons pure maple syrup (optional)
sparkling water

Place the sage leaves, apricots, filtered water and maple syrup into a blender and blend until smooth. Strain through a fine sieve (strainer) and pour into 4 serving glasses. Top up with sparkling water, stir and serve.

Pictured (text on opposite page): Hot Penicillin

GOJI TART WITH PASSION FRUIT CURD

MAKES 35 X 12CM (14 X 4½IN)

For the passion fruit curd

60ml (2fl oz/¼ cup) lemon juice

120ml (4fl oz/½ cup) passion fruit pulp (approximately 4 large passion fruit)

200g (7oz/generous ½ cup) raw honey

100ml (3½fl oz/scant ½ cup) fresh orange juice

5 egg yolks

2 tablespoons cornflour (cornstarch)

2 tablespoons extra-virgin olive oil

3 vegetarian gelatine leaves, soaked in cold water

For the goji tart case

125g (4oz/1 cup) goji berries, soaked in hot filtered water for 2 hours

300g (11oz/2 cups) raw macadamia nuts or cashews, soaked in filtered water for 2 hours

150g (5oz/1⅔ cups) desiccated (dry unsweetened) coconut

1 tablespoon vanilla extract

30g (1oz/3 tablespoons) chia seeds

For the filling, bring a small saucepan filled halfway with water to a simmer. Whisk the lemon juice, passion fruit pulp, honey, orange juice and eggs yolks together in a heatproof bowl and place the bowl over the simmering water. Make sure the bottom of the bowl doesn't touch the water's surface.

Whisk continuously for 6–7 minutes while the liquid heats and turns from sloshy and translucent to opaque. When you start to see steam rising from the liquid, scoop 4 tablespoons out of the bowl and whisk together with the cornflour.

Return the cornflour-infused liquid to the bowl and continue to whisk for 3–4 minutes more until the liquid thickens into a curd. Be careful not to let it come to a full simmer, or you'll start to scramble the eggs.

Remove from the heat and whisk in the olive oil and finally the soaked gelatine leaves until dissolved. Cover the filling with clingfilm (plastic wrap) and place in the refrigerator to completely cool.

In the meantime make the tart case. Place the drained goji berries and macadamia nuts, desiccated coconut and vanilla extract into a food processor and blend until a soft cookie dough-like texture is reached. Remove from the food processor and stir through the chia seeds. Allow to stand, uncovered, for 30 minutes. Line a tart tin (pan) or 23cm (9in) round tart tin with clingfilm (plastic wrap). Using a spatula, press the dough evenly into the tart tin. Refrigerate the tart case uncovered, until ready to fill.

To assemble the tart, remove the tart case from the refrigerator and spread the passion fruit curd into the goji berry tart case using a large dessertspoon and spatula. Refrigerate overnight before serving. This tart will keep in the refrigerator for up to 3 days.

APPLE SPICE ICE-CREAM (V)

SERVES 6–8

The key to this ice-cream is to make sure the apples are cooked all the way through. Making sure the apples are soft and tender will create a smooth texture to this ice-cream.

650g (1lb 7oz) apples, peeled
   and cored
¼ teaspoon sea salt
1 tablespoon melted coconut oil
1 tablespoon ground cinnamon
½ teaspoon ground cardamom
1 teaspoon ground ginger
½ teaspoon ground star anise
½ teaspoon ground nutmeg
1 whole vanilla pod (bean), seeds
   scraped
90g (3¼oz/¼ cup) pure maple syrup
800ml (27fl oz/3¼ cups) coconut milk
55g (2oz/⅓ cup) hazelnuts (filberts),
   roasted and roughly chopped

Chop the apples into bite-sized pieces. Place the coconut oil in a large saucepan over a low–medium heat. Add the chopped apples, salt, all the spices including the vanilla seeds and the empty pod. Add 2 tablespoons of the maple syrup, stir well and cook for 10 minutes or so, until the apples are soft. Allow to cool for 20 minutes.

Remove the vanilla pod from the saucepan, then place the apple mixture, the remaining 2 tablespoons maple syrup and the coconut milk into a food processor and process until smooth.

Either add this mixture to an ice-cream maker and churn until frozen or line a large loaf tin (pan) or glass baking dish with clingfilm (plastic wrap), making sure there is enough clingfilm hanging over the edges to cover the top as well. I like to use loaf tins (pans) or toughened glass dishes, as I find that plastic boxes sometimes crack when serving. Pour the mixture into the lined baking dish, cover and place in the freezer. When it is semi-solid (after 2–3 hours), whisk it again with a fork or spoon to break up the ice crystals and refreeze. Make sure the ice-cream is covered each time it goes into the freezer as ice crystals will form and create an icy cream instead of a smooth consistency. When just frozen, fold in the roasted chopped hazelnuts. Cover the ice-cream with clingfilm and place in the freezer to harden completely.

Remove the ice-cream at least 15 minutes before serving to soften.

Calm

This chapter is based on the sixth chakra, which is also known as the third eye, the organ of inner perception, where wisdom and intuition are formed. Opening our third eye allows us to see the bigger picture, to find wholeness, bringing with it both meaning and purpose. While each chakra feeds us new information about ourselves, it is the task of the sixth chakra to assemble that information into a recognisable picture. This self-reflection and deeper inner-knowledge leads to a wholeness within ourselves.

Many of the ingredients in this chapter include mood-enhancing foods such as matcha and raw cacao. Ingredients which help with our concentration, memory and focus are also prominent as are foods designed to nurture the nervous system, such as chamomile, lemon verbena and black sesame seeds.

It's in this chapter that an understanding of our true health can be found. No longer concerned by mere symptoms, our minds are able to process and see the body as a complete system. Reaching this place in our yogic evolution means that we are able to finally listen to what our bodies need and act accordingly.

SAVOURY FLAPJACKS

MAKES 12 FLAPACKS

This flapjack really hits the spot when you're craving something savoury, but light. A great on-the-go snack that tastes remarkably like a pizza slice. Feel free to play around with the ingredients here, you can substitute the courgettes (zucchini) for carrots and feta for goat's cheese if you prefer.

1 tablespoon coconut oil
1 small red onion, finely chopped
1 red (bell) pepper, diced
2 courgettes (zucchini), grated
3 tablespoons Kalamata olives, pitted
2 eggs, lightly whisked
50ml (1¾fl oz/scant ¼ cup) olive oil
250g (9oz/2½ cups) gluten-free rolled
    oats or millet flakes
1½ teaspoons dried oregano
1 teaspoon sea salt
½ teaspoon freshly cracked black
    pepper
150g (5oz/1 cup) crumbled feta

Preheat the oven to 180°C fan/400°F/ Gas 6. Line a 36 x 20cm (14 x 8in) square baking tin (pan) with baking paper (parchment paper). Place the coconut oil in a frying pan over a medium heat, add the onion and red pepper and sauté until soft. Add the courgettes and olives and cook for a further few minutes.

Transfer to a large mixing bowl and add the eggs, olive oil, oats, oregano, salt and pepper. Using your hands, mix to combine, then transfer to the prepared tin.

Add the crumbled feta over the top of the mixture and, using your hands or a flat spatula, pat the mixture firmly down into the baking tin. Sprinkle with a little more dried oregano.

Bake in the oven for 35 minutes or until golden and cooked through. Allow to cool before cutting into 12 squares.

Pictured L–R (text on page 148): Cacao Tahini Energy Balls, Black Sesame Mylk (text on page 156) and Matcha, Coconut & Lime Balls

MATCHA, COCONUT & LIME BALLS (V)

MAKES 18

Energy balls are great, mini, on-the-go snacks. Popular among yogis, these balls are a brilliant energy boosting snack before a yoga class.

120g (4oz/1½ cups) desiccated (dry unsweetened) coconut, plus 2 tablespoons extra for coating
85g (3oz/¾ cup) ground almonds
2 tablespoons melted coconut oil
3 tablespoons coconut nectar (for vegans) or raw honey
finely grated zest and juice of 2 limes
pinch of sea salt
1 teaspoon premium-grade matcha powder

Place all the ingredients in a food processor and process until the ingredients come together to form a dough. You can add more ground almonds or a dash of coconut oil depending if the mixture is too wet or dry.

Remove the mixture from the food processor and place in a medium bowl. Cover with clingfilm (plastic wrap) and refrigerate for 30 minutes. Once firmed, roll walnut-sized portions of the mixture in the palm of your hand. Place in a lock-seal bag with the 2 extra tablespoons of desiccated coconut. Seal the bag then shake to coat each ball in the coconut. Store in the airtight bag or another airtight container in the refrigerator. They will keep in an airtight container for 2 weeks.

CACAO TAHINI ENERGY BALLS (V)

MAKES 12 BALLS

65g (2¼oz/¼ cup) tahini paste
350g (12oz/2 cups) stoned (pitted) dried dates
30g (1oz/¼ cup) raw cacao powder
2 teaspoons sesame seeds

Place the tahini paste, dates and cacao powder into a food processor and blend. Have a taste of the mixture and adjust by adding more tahini if necessary. The mixture should be smooth with a hint of nuttiness.

Once the dates have combined with the other ingredients and turned into a smooth paste, remove the mixture from the food processor, scraping as much as possible away from the blade and food processor and place in medium bowl. Cover with plastic wrap and refrigerate for 30 minutes.

Roll the mixture into small balls and place in a lock-seal bag with the sesame seeds. Seal the bag then shake to coat each ball in the sesame seeds. Store in the airtight bag or another airtight container in the refrigerator. They will keep in an airtight container for 2 weeks.

MATCHAROONS

(V) MAKES 30

Matcha has become a popular food ingredient and its health benefits are ones I love to shout about. Matcha is bitter so when cooking use light flavours such as ginger, lime or cardamom to boost and enhance its flavour.

250g (9oz/2¾ cups) desiccated (dry unsweetened) coconut
2 tablespoons premium-grade matcha powder
1 tablespoon ground cardamom
250g (9oz/2½ cups) ground almonds
½ teaspoon Himalayan salt
260g (9½oz/¾ cup) coconut nectar (for vegans) or raw honey
75ml (2½fl oz/scant ⅓ cup) melted coconut oil
1 tablespoon vanilla extract

Preheat the oven to 120°C fan/275°F/Gas 1. Line 2 baking sheets with baking paper (parchment paper). In a large bowl, combine the coconut, matcha powder, ground cardamom, ground almonds and salt and stir to combine thoroughly. Add the coconut nectar, coconut oil and vanilla extract and stir well again. Chill in the refrigerator for 30 minutes.

Roll a small handful of the chilled mixture into a cookie-sized round in the palm of your hands, then place on the prepared baking sheet. Repeat with the remaining dough to make 30 cookies. Alternatively, use an ice-cream scoop to place even mounds onto the baking sheets. Flatten each cookie with the tines of a fork. These cookies do not spread while baking, so there is no need to space them too far apart.

Bake for 50–60 minutes or until dried and crisp around the edges but still soft in the middle. Remove from the oven and allow to cool on the baking sheets. They will keep in an airtight container for to 2 weeks.

KALE RIBS WITH BLUEBERRY, FETA & HAZELNUT SALSA

SERVES 4

This dish is so easy to prepare and such a flavour hit. Never one to throw away food, I was always intrigued by what I could do with the stalks of kale when I made kale crisps (chips).

For the dressing
3 tablespoons hemp oil
juice of 1 lime
2 tablespoons pure maple syrup or coconut nectar
freshly cracked black pepper

For the blueberry salsa
200g (7oz/1¼ cups) blueberries
200g (7oz/scant 1½ cups) hazelnuts (filberts), toasted and roughly chopped
100g (3½oz/scant ¾ cup) crumbled feta
large bunch of mint, leaves picked, finely chopped
large bunch of coriander (cilantro), finely chopped

For the kale ribs
25 whole kale leaves (or either cavolo nero or asparagus spears)
2 tablespoons coconut oil
pinch of Himalayan sea salt
freshly cracked black pepper
4 tablespoons black olive paste (available from good supermarkets)

To make the dressing, whisk all the ingredients together in a small bowl and set aside.

In a separate bowl, toss the blueberries with the chopped toasted hazelnuts, crumbled feta, mint and coriander. Pour half the dressing over and set aside.

Cut or tear all the green leaves off the kale stalks. Place the stalks (ribs) in a hot frying pan with the coconut oil, a sprinkling of Himalayan salt and some freshly cracked black pepper. Toss over a high heat until browned and blistered. Remove from the heat.

To assemble, place a tablespoon of black olive paste in the centre of the plate, then place approximately 5–7 ribs in the centre of each serving plate. Spoon the blueberry mixture over the kale ribs, then drizzle the remaining dressing over and serve immediately.

CAULIFLOWER WITH GRAPES, HAZELNUTS, & ALLSPICE (V)

SERVES 2

At first glance, purple sprouted cauliflower may look like a GMO-Frankenstein experiment gone wrong. However, in reality, it's simply a different variety of the common white cauliflower, only packed with anthocyanin, the same healthy antioxidant found in red wine. Anthocyanin-rich foods such as red cabbage, blueberries and purple sprouted cauliflower help to improve cognitive function and memory, especially in the elderly. They also have many cancer-fighting properties and lower the risk of cardiovascular disease due to their antioxidant-rich nutrients.

For the dressing
120g (4oz/½ cup) coconut yoghurt
¼ teaspoon ground cinnamon
¼ teaspoon allspice
1 tablespoon sherry vinegar
1 tablespoon pure maple syrup
¼ teaspoon sea salt

For the salad
1 large (900g/2lb) purple cauliflower
    head, (if purple cauliflowers are
    unavailable, use a white one)
    broken into bite-sized florets
½ small red onion, finely sliced
2 sprigs of dill (dillweed), roughly
    chopped, plus extra to garnish
100g (3½oz/generous ½ cup) red
    grapes, halved and seeded,
    if necessary
40g (1½oz/⅓ cup) hazelnuts (filberts),
    toasted and roughly chopped

For the dressing, place all the ingredients in a small bowl and whisk together. Adjust according to your taste.

In a large mixing bowl, mix the raw cauliflower florets, onion slices and dill. Pour the dressing over and toss to coat all the florets. Add the grapes to the mixing bowl. Place the salad on a serving platter and sprinkle with the chopped hazelnuts and extra dill leaves to serve.

WALDORF SALAD (V)

SERVES 4

For the dressing
2 tablespoons pomegranate molasses
60ml (2fl oz/¼ cup) extra-virgin
 olive oil
juice of 1 large lemon

For the salad
¼ red cabbage, thinly sliced using
 a mandolin
3 large celery stalks, washed and cut
 into long, diagonal, thin slices
2 Granny Smith apples, cored and
 thinly sliced into rounds
4–6 radishes, thinly sliced
½ large fennel bulb, trimmed and then
 thinly sliced using a mandolin
100g (3½oz/generous ½ cup) red
 grapes, halved, and seeded, if
 necessary
2 red chicory (Belgian endive) heads,
 leaves separated
small bunch of flat-leaf parsley,
 roughly chopped
roughly crushed walnuts and
 pomegranate seeds, to garnish

Place all the dressing ingredients in a small mixing bowl and whisk to combine. Set aside.

Place all the prepared vegetables in a large mixing bowl and toss together using your hands. Once combined, drizzle the dressing over the salad, then toss together once again, making sure all the ingredients are coated.

Place the salad on a serving platter and garnish with some crushed walnuts and pomegranate seeds.

BALSAMIC ROASTED RED ONIONS, AUBERGINE, FIG & OLIVE SALAD (V)

SERVES 4

The sweetness of the balsamic really brings out the wonderful flavour of the onions. You can prepare the onions for this salad a few hours before you need them – or even the day before – which only heightens their flavour.

2 large red onions
60ml (2fl oz/¼ cup) good-quality
    balsamic vinegar
2 tablespoons filtered water
2 large aubergines (eggplants), cut into
    large chunks
2–3 tablespoons olive oil
sea salt and freshly cracked black
    pepper
50g (2oz/⅓ cup) raw whole almonds
60g (2¼oz) radicchio leaves, roughly
    torn
40g (1½oz/1 cup) rocket (arugula)
    leaves
large bunch of basil, leaves chopped
4 large red figs, roughly torn into
    bite-sized pieces
50g (2oz/scant ½ cup) pitted black
    olives, of your choice

Preheat the oven to 210°C fan/475°F/ Gas 9. Trim the root end of each onion, trying to keep a little intact so the onions will hold together when cut. Cut the onions in half and then peel the skin off. Cut the halves into 2 or 3 wedges depending on the size. Place the onions, balsamic vinegar and the filtered water in a baking tray, toss gently and roast in the hot oven for 20 minutes. You will need to keep checking the onions don't burn and cover loosely with foil if over-browning. When the onions are soft, remove from the oven.

In the meantime, place the aubergine chunks on a baking tray (baking sheet). Drizzle with the olive oil and season with salt and pepper. Toss then roast in the hot oven at the same time as the onions for 25 minutes or until soft and golden brown. Remove from the oven and reduce the oven temperature to 160°C fan/350°F/Gas 4.

Spread out the almonds on a small baking tray and place in the oven for 20 minutes. Remove from the oven and, when cool enough to handle, roughly chop.

In a large mixing bowl, mix the radicchio, rocket and basil leaves together, then toss through the roasted onions, aubergine and figs. Scatter with the chopped almonds and olives. Season with sea salt and freshly cracked black pepper and serve.

CACAO & CREAM SMOOTHIE

(V) SERVES 2

Perfect for those indulgent morning smoothie moments.

1 tablespoon raw cacao powder
2 bananas
1 tablespoon hemp protein
1 teaspoon ground cinnamon
500ml (17fl oz/2¼ cups) almond milk

Blend all the ingredients together in a blender for 2–3 minutes. Pour into glasses and enjoy.

BLACK SESAME MYLK (V)

MAKES 750ML (25FL OZ/ GENEROUS 1 CUP)

Sesame seeds are wonderful little seeds which contain high levels of calcium. They also hold an impressive amount of magnesium which together with vitamin D is essential for calcium absorption. Magnesium also stimulates our calitonin production. Calitonin is a hormone that makes calcium stay in the bones thus keeping it from being absorbed into the soft tissues. Calcium and magnesium have a very calming effect on the body and can be effectively used as a treatment for insomnia or anxiety.

There is a major difference between the calcium content of hulled versus unhulled sesame seeds. When using unhulled seeds, 1 tablespoon of sesame seeds will contains about 88mg of calcium. When the hulls are removed, this same tablespoon will contain about 5-10mg (about 90-95% less).

160g (5½oz/generous 1 cup) black unhulled sesame seeds (or whole white sesame seeds)
1 teaspoon lemon juice
700ml (22fl oz/2¾ cups) filtered water, plus extra for soaking
3 Medjool dates
1 teaspoon ground cardamom

Place the sesame seeds in a medium bowl, add the lemon juice and cover with enough filtered water to come 1cm (½in) above the seeds. Soak for 8 hours or overnight, then rinse thoroughly and drain.

Place the soaked and drained sesame seeds, the measured water, dates and cardamom in a high-speed blender and blend for 2–3 minutes.

If you would like your sesame milk to be silky smooth and pulp free, pour the sesame milk through a nut milk bag or muslin (cheesecloth) and remove the pulp. If so, add the dates and cardamom after you have strained the milk and re-blend.

COCONUT, GINGER & MISO ICE-CREAM (V)

SERVES 6

This vegan ice-cream is the real deal. The secret is nothing more than full-fat, creamy coconut milk. Other vegan milk substitutes, like almond, rice or soy milk, just don't cut it when it comes to ice-cream.

800ml (27fl oz/3¼ cups) full-fat
    coconut milk
1 tablespoon arrowroot
120ml (4fl oz/½ cup) pure maple syrup
5cm (2in) piece of fresh ginger,
    peeled and cut into thin slices
1 tablespoon white miso paste

In a small bowl, whisk together 200ml (7fl oz/scant 1 cup) of the coconut milk and the arrowroot until smooth. Set aside.

Place the remaining coconut milk, the maple syrup, fresh ginger and miso paste in a medium saucepan over a low heat. Whisk to ensure the miso is thoroughly incorporated. Bring to the moment just before it begins to boil then add the whisked coconut milk and arrowroot mixture. This will thicken the mixture. Remove from the heat and keep stirring until thick and creamy and all the ingredients are incorporated. Cover and allow to infuse until cold.

Before freezing or placing liquid into an ice-cream machine, strain the liquid through a fine sieve and discard the contents of the sieve.

Either add the strained liquid to an ice-cream maker and churn until frozen or line a large loaf tin (pan) or glass baking dish with plastic wrap, making sure there is enough plastic wrap hanging over the edges to cover the top as well. Pour the mixture into the lined baking dish, cover, and place in the freezer. When it is semi-solid (after 2–3 hours), whisk it again with a fork or spoon to break up the ice crystals and refreeze. Make sure the ice-cream is covered each time it goes into the freezer as ice crystals will form and create an 'icy' ice-cream instead of a smooth, creamy consistency. When frozen, place in a food processor or blender and process until smooth. Cover and refreeze until ready to serve.

BERRIED ALIVE ICE-CREAM WITH BAOBAB (V)

SERVES 2–4

More of a sorbet in appearance, this ice-cream is smooth and creamy. With the added hidden benefits of baobab, this ice-cream packs a real vitamin C punch. If your raspberries are too tart, you may like to add more vanilla bean paste.

500g (1lb/2oz) fresh or frozen raspberries
160ml (5fl oz/⅔ cup) coconut cream
2 tablespoons baobab powder
1 tablespoon vanilla bean paste

Place the frozen raspberries, coconut cream, baobab powder and vanilla paste into a high-speed blender or food processor. It is not necessary to have an ice-cream machine to make wonderful ice-creams or sorbets, but they do create the best results.

Transfer the mixture to ice-cream maker and process according to manufacturer's instructions, churning for approximately 1 hour.

Alternatively, line a baking dish with clingfilm (plastic wrap) making sure there is enough clingfilm hanging over the edges to cover the top as well. I like to use loaf tins (pans) or glass dishes, as plastic containers tend to crack upon serving. Pour the mixture into the lined baking dish, cover and place in the freezer for 2-3 hours. When it is semi-solid, whisk it again with a fork or spoon and refreeze. Make sure the ice-cream is covered each time it goes into the freezer as ice crystals will form and create an 'icy' ice-cream instead of a smooth, creamy consistency. When frozen, place in a food processor or blender and process until smooth. Cover and refreeze until serving time.

Feel free to use any berries or fruits to begin creating wonderful creamy ice-creams.

CHAMOMILE & PLUM TART (V)

MAKES 32 X 12CM TART (12½ X 4½IN)

Soothing in its approach, chamomile is a herb I commonly use to mildly sedate and calm the body. Effective at inducing a relaxing sleep for insomnia due to its muscle relaxant and sedative properties and when used in food, chamomile has a very calming effect on digestion, helping to relieve bloating, nausea or any cramping pains.

You can also use peaches or even apricots as a substitute for the plums.

6–8 ripe plums (depending on size), halved and stoned (pitted)

For the filling
350ml (12fl oz/1½ cups) boiling filtered water
3 chamomile tea bags
275g (10oz/1¾ cups) raw cashews
3 tablespoons pure maple syrup
2 teaspoons vanilla extract
pinch of salt

For the coconut macadamia tart case
85g (3oz/scant 1 cup) desiccated (dry unsweetened) coconut
200g (7oz/1½ cups) raw macadamia nuts
60ml (2fl oz/¼ cup) pure maple syrup
pinch of sea salt

For the plums, preheat the oven to 210°C fan/450°F/Gas 9. Line a baking tray (baking sheet) with baking paper (parchment paper). Place the plums, cut side down, on the tray and bake for 10 minutes, then remove from the oven and turn the plums over. Return to the oven and roast for 10 minutes or until the plums are soft. Remove from the oven and allow to cool.

To make the filling, in a medium heatproof bowl, pour the boiling water over the chamomile tea bags and cover with foil. Set aside and allow to cool completely. Add the cashews and leave to soak for 2 hours, or overnight if more convenient. Once the cashews have soaked, drain the chamomile tea into a small jug (pitcher), discarding the tea bags. Place the cashews, maple syrup, vanilla, salt and 60ml (2fl oz/¼ cup) of the reserved chamomile tea in a high-speed blender or small food processor and blend until a smooth cream-like consistency is reached.

For the tart base, place all the ingredients into the food processor, add 2 tablespoons of the remaining chamomile tea and blend until a soft cookie dough-like texture is reached. Add a splash more tea if too dry. Line a 23cm (9in) loose-bottomed tart tin (pan) with clingfilm (plastic wrap). Using a spatula and your hands, press the dough evenly into the tart tin and chill to firm for at least 30 minutes.

To assemble the tart, remove the tart case from the refrigerator and gently spread the cashew cream into the tart case with a large dessertspoon and spatula. Place the roasted plums, cut side up, over the cashew filling.

This tart will keep in the refrigerator for up to 3 days.

RHUBARB, BLUEBERRY & LEMON VERBENA CHIA JAM (V)

MAKES 800ML (27FL OZ/ 3½ CUPS)

You can buy liquorice powder from good health food stores and online. Feel free to use any berries or fruits to create this wonderful jam.

500g (1lb 2oz) rhubarb, washed, trimmed and sliced into 2–3cm (¾–1in) pieces
500g (1lb 2oz/3⅓ cups) blueberries
2 tablespoons lemon juice
6 sprigs of lemon verbena (or if fresh is unavailable use a lemon verbena tea bag)
2–3 teaspoons raw liquorice powder
120g (4oz/generous 1 cup) chia seeds

Place the rhubarb, blueberries, lemon juice and lemon verbena in a medium saucepan over a medium heat. Using a wooden spoon, slowly start to break the fruit down as it begins to soften. As soon as the fruit has broken down and is cooked, (after about 10–12 minutes) remove from the heat. Allow to cool for 15 minutes, then add the liquorice powder and whisk to combine. Taste and if you need a little more sweetness, add more liquorice powder.

Add the chia seeds and thoroughly whisk again to combine, making sure the chia seeds have not clumped together anywhere in the saucepan. Allow the jam to stand until cold, while the chia seeds absorb the juices and thicken. Carefully pour the jam into clean screw-topped jars and store in the refrigerator for up to 2 weeks.

MOCHA PANNA COTTA WITH ROASTED FIGS (V)

SERVES 4

This mocha version is seductively charismatic but won't leave you feeling guilty despite its indulgent appearance. If figs are not in season, try other seasonal fruit such as plums or early summer cherries.

For the panna cotta
100ml (3½fl oz/scant ½ cup) filtered water
1 sachet Vege-Gel powder (or another vegetarian gelatine substitute)
350ml (12fl oz/1½ cups) almond milk
2 teaspoons vanilla bean paste
20g (¾oz/⅛ cup) raw cacao powder
double shot espresso coffee
    (or ½ teaspoon instant coffee)
100g (4oz/½ cup) coconut sugar

For the roasted figs
4 figs
2 tablespoons maple syrup
1 teaspoon vanilla extract

Place the filtered water in a small bowl. Add the Vege-Gel powder and stir until the powder is dissolved. Set aside.

Pour the almond milk into a medium saucepan over a low–medium heat and add the vanilla paste, cacao powder, espresso coffee and coconut sugar. Stir constantly until the sugar is dissolved and the cacao powder is incorporated.

Stir in the Vege-Gel liquid and bring it to the point just before the milk boils. Remove from the heat immediately. Strain the liquid through a fine sieve (strainer) into a pouring jug (pitcher). Pour the panna cotta mixture into 4 ramekins (custard cups) or serving glasses of your choice. Leave to cool completely and then refrigerate for 3–4 hours or until set.

Preheat the oven to 180°C fan/400°F/Gas 6. Line a baking tray (baking sheet) with baking paper (parchment paper). Cut each fig in half and place on the baking tray. Drizzle with the maple syrup and vanilla extract and roast in the oven for 10–15 minutes or until the figs are golden and soft. This will take varying lengths of time due to how ripe your figs are. Remove from the oven once roasted and allow to cool in their juices.

To serve the panna cotta, turn the moulds out onto plates and serve with 2 roasted fig halves and a drizzle of the figs roasting juices.

MATCHA CHIA PUDDING (V)

SERVES 2-4

Packed full of antioxidants and green goodness this breakfast chia pudding will give you all the energy you need for the day ahead. Perfect for a morning pick-me-up, matcha not only releases energy throughout the day it also boosts your mood and aids concentration.

For the chia pudding
1 teaspoon premium-grade matcha powder
200ml (7fl oz/scant 1 cup) unsweetened almond milk
1 tablespoon pure maple syrup or coconut nectar
2 tablespoons chia seeds

For the layers
100g (3½oz/2⅔ cups) coconut yoghurt
100g (3½oz/1 cup) Kaleola (see page 96)
100g (3½oz/⅔ cup) blueberries
2 tablespoons hazelnut (filbert) butter (see page 19)
Cacao nibs and bee pollen, to decorate

Begin by making the chia pudding. Using a bamboo matcha tea whisk or a small wire or silicone whisk, create a paste with the matcha powder and 2 teaspoons of the almond milk. Once a paste is formed, whisk in the remaining almond milk and maple syrup. Add the chia seeds and whisk once more to combine. Cover with clingfilm (plastic wrap) and allow to set for 2 hours in the refrigerator. To assemble the pudding, you may need to add a little more almond milk to loosen the chia pudding.

To serve, take 2 serving glasses and divide the coconut yoghurt at the bottom of each glass, then sprinkle the Kaleola over the yoghurt. Divide the blueberries over the Kaleola, then spoon 2 tablespoons of the chia pudding over the blueberries. Place a tablespoon of hazelnut butter on top of the chia pudding, then sprinkle with cacao nibs and bee pollen.

CHOCOLATE SPICED CHIA COOKIES (V)

MAKES 20

More of a macaroon, these cookies aren't your traditional cookie. Egg has been replaced by chia seeds as the binding agent, so be sure to allow enough time for the seeds to absorb the liquids to help bind the cookies. If you find they won't stick together, add a little more chia and allow to soak for 10 minutes longer until the dough sticks together.

250g (9oz/2¾ cups) desiccated (dry unsweetened) coconut
40g (1½oz/¼ cup) chia seeds
120g (4oz/1 cup) raw cacao powder
50g (2oz/½ cup) ground almonds
½ teaspoon fine Himalayan salt
1 teaspoon ground cinnamon
½ teaspoon ground ginger
½ teaspoon ground cardamom
pinch of ground cloves
75ml (2½fl oz/scant ⅓ cup) filtered water
260g (9½oz/¾ cup) pure maple syrup or coconut nectar
75ml (2½fl oz/scant ⅓ cup) melted coconut oil
1 tablespoon vanilla extract

Preheat the oven to 120°C fan/275°F/ Gas 1. Line 2 baking trays (baking sheets) with baking paper (parchment paper). In a large bowl, combine the desiccated coconut, chia seeds, cacao powder, ground almonds, salt, spices and water and mix thoroughly. Add the maple syrup, coconut oil and vanilla extract and stir again until fully combined. Cover with clingfilm (plastic wrap) and chill in the refrigerator for 30 minutes.

Once ready to bake, roll a small handful of the chilled mixture into a cookie-like round, then place on the prepared baking sheets. Alternatively, use an ice-cream scoop to place even amounts onto the sheets. These cookies do not spread while baking, so there is no need to space them too far apart. Flatten each cookie with the tines of a fork.

Bake in the oven for 50–60 minutes or until dried and crisp around the edges but still soft in the middle. Remove from the oven and allow to cool on the baking sheets. Store in an airtight container.

Pure

This chapter is based on the final crown chakra, which focuses on understanding our true nature, where all is pure, simple and intentional.

The brain, in terms of nutrient needs, is the greediest organ in our bodies and as the primary survival organ it demands nutrients before any other organ. When well-nourished, our brain will allow the rest of the body to flourish; so, it makes perfect sense to nourish the brain optimally as this leads to an advanced overall health status. Eating a diet rich in organic nuts, seeds and unprocessed oils, as well as lots of green leafy vegetables, provides both Omega-3 and Omega-6 fatty acids. These recipes contain a great deal of Omega-3-rich ingredients such as hemp, chia and ground flaxseeds, as well as a premium selection of essential fatty acid oils to build, detoxify and support your brain.

In the crown chakra we explore our universal identity, where inter-connection and spirit are finally accessible to us. We seek purity and accept oxygen and sunlight as foods for our soul. We should naturally gravitate towards organic produce, eco-friendly homes and non-GMO foods. Fasting and detoxification become normal practice as a way of staying 'pure', so this chapter focuses on food which detoxifies the body, making us feel 'light' and deeply connected to ourselves and the outer world.

BREAKFAST SANGUINE SALAD (V)

SERVES 2–4

This sanguine salad is the purest way to start your day. Designed to kick-start your liver and digestion, the freshly bitter flavours of the pomelo and grapefruit combined with the carminative herbs of fennel, mint and basil will guarantee your liver and digestion are awake and ready for the day ahead. This delicate dish is a simple way to cleanse each morning.

2 pink grapefruits
2 pomelos or large yellow grapefruits
2 blood oranges
3 clementines, peeled
seeds from ½ pomegranate
finely grated zest and juice of ½ lime
3 sprigs of mint, leaves picked
3 sprigs of basil, leaves picked
2 fennel herb fronds, roughly chopped,
    discarding central stalk

Begin by peeling the pink grapefruits, pomelos and blood oranges. Using a sharp, preferably serrated knife, cut the bottom and top off each fruit, then slice the knife down the side of each fruit between the pith and the flesh all round, removing all the pith with the peel. Cut each fruit into quarters lengthways, then cut each quarter into segments making sure to cut in between the membranes of each segment. Remove any pips (seeds) as you go. This will be a very juicy process. Make sure to keep the juices by placing in a large bowl, along with all the fruit segments.

Now pull the individual clementine pieces apart and, using the same sharp knife, cut each segment in half lengthways. Place in the large bowl along with the other fruit. Add the pomegranate seeds, lime zest and juice, mint, basil leaves and fennel fronds, toss together and serve immediately.

ZA'ATAR GREEN CABBAGE CRISPS

SERVES 2 AS A SNACK

Crisps (chips) are going through a renaissance as they've become a popular makeover dish for health-conscious foodies everywhere. No root vegetable or kale leaf has been left unshaved in this race, but in this recipe I have decided to use another one of the brassica family vegetables and offer a different kind of crisp. I love the texture of the Savoy cabbage, because the surface of the leaves aren't smooth, the crisps have an added crunch when they're cooked. If you don't want to spice with za'atar, which you can make yourself or buy in all good supermarkets, you could simply sprinkle a little paprika or sumac and dried oregano over the top before baking.

4–5 outer leaves of Savoy cabbage
1 tablespoon extra-virgin olive oil
1½ tablespoons za'atar spice and
   herb mix (see page 76)
½ teaspoon Himalayan salt

Preheat the oven to 200°C fan/430°F/ Gas 7. Using a sharp knife, slice the stem out of each leaf. Tear the cabbage into haphazard shaped 5cm (2in) bite-sized pieces and add to a colander. Wash the leaves, drain and then dry thoroughly using a salad spinner or clean tea towel (dishtowel).

Place the dry, torn leaves into a medium mixing bowl. Add the olive oil and sprinkle with the za'atar and salt while tossing the cabbage to get an even coating of oil and spice. Line 2 baking trays (baking sheets) with baking paper (parchment paper). Place or spread out on the prepared baking trays and bake for 10–15 minutes. Check the crisps every 5 minutes to ensure they are baking evenly, giving them a slight toss together or turning each crisp over. You may need to remove some crisps from the oven earlier if they are not baking evenly. Remove from the oven and allow to cool. Serve once cooled or store in an airtight container.

SPICE-INFUSED POMELO SALAD (V)

SERVES 4

For the marinade

50ml (2fl oz/¼ cup) mirin
50ml (2fl oz/¼ cup) orange juice
1 tablespoon orange blossom water
1 cardamom pod
1 star anise
1 cinnamon stick
2cm (¾in) piece of fresh ginger, peeled and cut into thin slices
½ teaspoon Thai green curry paste (optional)

For the salad

1 large pomelo (about 350g/12oz peeled weight) or large grapefruit if pomelo is unavailable, peeled
100g (3½oz) mangetout (snow peas), cut into thin strips
½ red (bell) pepper, julienned
100g (3½oz/generous ½ cup) shelled fresh or frozen edamame beans
4 spring onions (scallions), trimmed and diagonally sliced
100g (3½oz/generous 1 cup) bean sprouts, washed
handful of coriander (cilantro) leaves
handful of mint leaves, roughly chopped
juice of 2 limes
2 tablespoons toasted coconut flakes
2 tablespoons roasted cashews
lime wedges, to garnish
½ teaspoon chilli flakes, to garnish

Start by making the marinade. Place the mirin and orange juice in a saucepan over a low heat and warm gently. Remove from the heat and add the orange blossom water, cardamom, star anise, cinnamon, ginger and Thai curry paste, if using. Stir through and set aside to infuse.

Cut the pomelo in half, separate into segments then, holding the segments over a shallow bowl to catch the juice, carefully remove and discard the membranes. Break the flesh into bite-sized pieces and place in the bowl. Pour the marinade over the flesh and leave for 20–30 minutes – the longer the better.

Remove and discard the cardamom, star anise and cinnamon. Drain and reserve the marinade juice.

Place the pomelo flesh in a large bowl along with the other salad ingredients, except the nuts and lime wedges. Pour the marinade juice over the salad and toss to coat all the ingredients. Place on a serving platter or individual plates and scatter with toasted coconut flakes and cashews. Garnish with wedges of lime to squeeze over and chilli flakes.

BEETROOT, PINK GRAPEFRUIT & GOAT'S CHEESE CARPACCIO

SERVES 4

2 tablespoons flaxseed oil
2 tablespoons za'atar spice mix (see page 76)
1 large red beetroot (beet), peeled and thinly sliced with a mandolin
1 large golden beetroot, peeled and thinly sliced with a mandolin
1 pink grapefruit, peeled and thinly sliced
4 thin goat's cheese slices, chilled
12 Kalamata olives, pitted
4 radishes, washed and sliced in half
a few rocket (arugula) leaves
1 tablespoon balsamic glaze
red chard or spinach leave (optional)

Using a pastry brush, brush ½ tablespoon of flaxseed oil over 4 serving plates. Sprinkle a little of the za'atar spice mix over the oil, then begin to layer the red and yellow beetroot and pink grapefruit slices over the plate.

Place 1 goat's cheese slice onto each plate, then scatter the olives, radish slices, rocket leaves over the plate. Add the balsamic glaze to the plate and scatter over a couple of red chard or spinach leaves. Serve immediately.

ROASTED FENNEL & LEMON SALAD WITH TURMERIC WALNUTS

SERVES 2–4

Fennel has to be one of my favourite vegetables. I love it mainly for its carminative effects but also for its distinctive aniseed flavour. However, once roasted, this aniseed flavour mellows leaving a beautifully delicate flavour which when combined with turmeric and lemon dazzle the palate. (The turmeric walnuts also make a great snack or accompaniment to other salads.)

For the walnuts
50g (2oz/scant ¼ cup) raw honey
pinch of chilli flakes
½ teaspoon ground turmeric
¼ teaspoon sea salt
100g (3½oz/1 cup) raw walnuts, halves

For the salad
2 lemons, halved lengthways, pips (seeds) removed and cut widthways into 2mm (¹⁄₁₆in) slices
4 fennel bulbs, trimmed and cut into wedges lengthways
1 tablespoon melted coconut oil
sea salt
50g (2oz/1 cup) pea shoots
handful of tarragon leaves, roughly chopped

Preheat the oven to 170°C fan/375°F/Gas 5. Line a baking tray (baking sheet) with baking paper (parchment paper). Place the honey, chilli flakes, turmeric and sea salt in a small bowl and whisk together adding a touch of water to help loosen and create a thick paste. Add the walnuts and stir until well coated. Spread the walnuts out on the prepared baking tray and roast in the oven for about 15–20 minutes or until golden and crunchy but still a little sticky. Remove from the oven and set aside.

Increase the oven temperature to 200°C fan/430°F/Gas 7. Bring a small saucepan of water to the boil, then add the lemon slices and blanch for 2 minutes. Drain well, then place the blanched lemon slices and the fennel wedges in a bowl with the 1 tablespoon of the coconut oil and a sprinkling of sea salt. Gently coat the lemon and fennel in the coconut oil and sea salt. Line 2 baking trays with baking paper. Place the mixture on the prepared baking trays and roast in the oven for roughly 20–25 minutes or until the lemons have dried out a little and the fennel is cooked through. Remove from the oven and allow to cool. You may like to cook the lemons a little longer if needed.

Toss the pea shoots and tarragon through the lemon and fennel pieces and serve scattered with the sticky turmeric walnuts.

CURE ME TEA (V)

**MAKES 1 LITRE
(34FL OZ/4¼ CUPS)**

If a 'cure me' regime is
really needed, then I
recommend you, ideally,
drink 2 litres (68fl oz/8½
cups) of this tea every day.
YEP or EPY tea is a blend
of yarrow, elderflower and
peppermint and is renowned
for its curative powers. It
is available online or from
specialist stores.

1 litre (34fl oz/4¼ cups) boiling
   filtered water
2cm (¾in) piece of fresh ginger,
   peeled and thinly sliced
2cm (¾in) piece of fresh turmeric,
   peeled and thinly sliced
   (or 1 teaspoon ground turmeric)
1 teaspoon coriander seeds
1 teaspoon cumin seeds
1 teaspoon fennel seeds
2 cardamom pods
1 heaped tablespoon YEP tea
   (use peppermint or green
   tea if unavailable)
½ lemon, sliced
1 teaspoon manuka honey

Place all the ingredients in a French
press teapot and allow to steep for
15 minutes before plunging. You can
refill the plunger one more time if
needed. Alternatively, simmer all the
ingredients together in a covered pan
for 15 minutes. Strain before drinking.

ALOE, GRAPEFRUIT & GINGER SHOTS (V)

MAKES 2 SHOTS

Drink this elixir each day and you
won't feel the need for coffee ever
again. You and your senses will feel
so alive and rejuvenated. The aloe
vera will detox and cleanse your
digestive system while the ginger
gets to work on balancing hormones
and removing inflammation from
your body. Enjoy the sweet bitterness
as the grapefruit gently wakes your
liver and prepares your digestion
for the day ahead.

½–1 pink grapefruit, peeled
2cm (¾in) piece of fresh ginger
30ml (1fl oz/2 tablespoons) aloe
   vera juice

Pass the grapefruit and ginger through
a juicer. Add the aloe vera and give a
gentle stir. Serve in shot glasses.

BEAUTY TONIC SMOOTHIE (V)

SERVES 2

If you are looking for a daily
smoothie to tonify your skin and
keep you hydrated, then this
smoothie ticks all your boxes. The
coconut water keeps your body
hydrated, while the essential fatty
acids found in the avocado and hemp
oil will hydrate your skin and offer
that glow and softness we all crave.

¼ fresh pineapple, peeled
flesh of 1 ripe avocado
1 tablespoon extra-virgin hemp oil
juice of 1 lime
500ml (17fl oz/2¼ cups)
   coconut water

Blend all the ingredients together in
a blender for 2–3 minutes. Pour into
2 glasses and enjoy.

Pictured L–R (text on page opposite): Beauty Tonic Smoothie, Cure Me Tea and Aloe Grapefruit & Ginger Shots

RAW CARAMEL SLICE WITH BEE POLLEN CRISPIES

MAKES 10 BARS

This recipe uses lecithin to help the caramel thicken. In cooking terms, lecithin is a lipid that is partially dissolvable in water and therefore used as an emulsifier to help blend and bind ingredients that don't normally mix. It is available as either soy or sunflower. Stay away from the soy variety, which is often subjected to genetic modification and chemical processes, and choose the sunflower lecithin as it is frequently organic and natural with no genetic engineering and is normally extracted by cold-pressing.

For the base
120g (4oz/scant 1 cup) raw hazelnuts (filberts), or nut of your choice
25g (1oz/¼ cup) desiccated (dry unsweetened) coconut
6 dates, stoned (pitted)
60ml (2fl oz/¼ cup) melted coconut oil

For the caramel
16 dates, stoned (pitted)
50g (2oz/¼ cup) almond butter (see page 19)
2 tablespoons pure maple syrup
2 tablespoons tahini paste
2 teaspoons vanilla bean paste
1 teaspoon ground cardamom
pinch of sea salt flakes
2 tablespoons sunflower lecithin

For the topping
20g (¾oz/scant ¼ cup) raw cacao powder
50ml (1¾fl oz/scant ¼ cup) melted coconut oil
120g (4oz/scant ¼ cup) rice malt syrup
3 tablespoons bee pollen granules

To make the base, place the hazelnuts, coconut, dates and oil in a food processor and process for 1–2 minutes or until the mixture resembles fine breadcrumbs. Press the mixture into the base of a 20cm (8in) lightly greased square baking tin (pan) lined with baking paper (parchment paper) and refrigerate for 2–3 hours until firm.

To make the caramel, place the dates, almond butter, maple syrup, tahini paste, vanilla, cardamom and salt in a food processor and process for 1–2 minutes or until smooth. Add the sunflower lecithin and blend again until incorporated. This should help to thicken the caramel. Spread over the prepared base and return to the refrigerator.

To make the topping, place the cacao, coconut oil and rice malt syrup in a heatproof bowl set over a saucepan of simmering water and stir for 2–3 minutes or until melted and smooth. Sprinkle the bee pollen granules over the caramel and gently pat down with a spatula. Pour the cacao mixture over the date caramel and leave to cool, then refrigerate for 2 hours or until set. Cut into bars to serve. Store any leftovers in an airtight container in the refrigerator.

MINTED PASSION FRUIT LOLLIES (V)

SERVES 6

pulp from 5 passion fruits
leaves from 2 sprigs of mint, washed
200g (7oz) fresh pineapple, peeled
    and roughly chopped
200ml (7fl oz/scant 1 cup) full-fat
    coconut milk

Begin by placing all the passion fruit pulp into a small bowl and give it a quick stir with a fork to ensure the flesh and seeds are not clumped together. Set aside.

Now place all the remaining ingredients in a high-speed blender and blend until smooth. (If using a regular blender, this may take 1 minute or longer).

For the fresh look of the passion fruit in these ice lollies (popsicles), place a little of the passion fruit pulp into each of 6 lolly moulds (molds), then pour a little of the blended pineapple mixture over the top. Alternate this process, filling all of the moulds. Make sure to leave a little space for the liquid to expand, then using a lolly stick or skewer, stir the liquids together slightly. Place a lolly stick in each mould and put in the freezer until completely frozen.

To remove, run the moulds under warm water until the seal is broken and the lollies slide out.

HOLISTIC DISPENSARY

BUCKWHEAT

Despite it's name, buckwheat is unrelated to wheat. It is a gluten-free seed that is inexpensive to buy and versatile to use. Often known as 'kasha' the raw whole seed 'groats' are perfect for making porridge (oatmeal), granola, risotto or salads and the flour can be used in gluten-free baking. Buckwheat is mild in flavour and great if you want to add a crunch factor. It is also high in protein, manganese and copper levels and can stabilise blood sugar levels so is good for diabetics.

MILLET

Another gluten-free seed, millet is creamy in texture and fluffy like rice. It feeds pathogenic yeast (candida), acts as a probiotic to feed important microflora in your inner-ecosystem, provides serotonin to calm and soothe your moods as well as helps you to hydrate your colon.

OATS

Oats gain part of their distinctive flavour from the roasting process that they undergo after being harvested and cleaned. Although oats are then hulled, this process does not strip away their bran and germ allowing them to retain a concentrated source of their fibre and nutrients. Oats also contain avenin, which is a protein similar to gluten. However, research has shown that most people with coeliac disease can safely eat avenin. Oats, via their high fibre content, are known to help remove cholesterol from the digestive system that would otherwise end up in the bloodstream, therefore being cardio-protective.

QUINOA

Available in white, black or red seeds, quinoa is a naturally gluten-free seed and contains iron, B-vitamins, magnesium, phosphorus, potassium, calcium, vitamin E and fibre. It is also one of a few plant foods that contains all nine essential amino acids, making it a complete protein. Available in various forms such as puffed, flaked, ground flour or the seed, this versatile ingredient can be used to make granola, risotto, porridge (oatmeal), baked dishes, salads, or as a starch substitute. Please rinse well before use as its saponin coating can be an irritant to the gut and creates a bitter flavour.

CHICKPEAS

They have a delicious nut-like taste and a texture that is buttery, yet somewhat starchy and pasty. A very versatile legume, chickpeas are high in fibre and protein and can boost your energy because of their high iron content. Also known as gram or besan, the flour can be used to make flatbreads or crackers.

COLD-PRESSED COCONUT OIL

Coconut oil is nature's richest source of medium-chain fatty acids. By contrast, most common vegetables or seed oils are comprised of long-chain fatty acids, also known as triglycerides or bad fats. Triglycerides are large molecules, so they are difficult for our body to break down and are predominantly stored as fat. But medium-chain fats, are smaller, and therefore easily digested and immediately burned by your liver for energy – like carbohydrates, but without the insulin spike. Coconut oil actually boosts your metabolism and helps your body use fat for energy. It is primarily a saturated fat, meaning when it is cooked it does not create a free-radical soup like it does with other vegetable oils. Coconut oil is the most stable of any known oils and is my preferred oil to cook with. Only buy extra-virgin varieties and ensure it has been cold-pressed.

Coconut oil is a saturated fat, however don't confuse this with other cheaper fats that have been saturated artificially through hydrogenation. True natural saturation of bonds encase the structure of coconut oil, which allows for the transport and delivery of the substance lauric acid which make up 50% of coconut oil. Lauric acid is anti-viral, anti-bacterial and also helps reverse the damage caused to blood viscosity by the multitude of polyunsaturated fats found in so many processed foods.

EXTRA-VIRGIN OLIVE OIL

Olive oil is a monounsaturated oil, which helps lower cholesterol by blocking cholesterol absorption from food. It has been proven to improve cardiovascular function, digestion by improving liver and gall bladder function and increases bile flow and stimulates pancreatic enzyme production. It also acts as an antioxidant, anti-inflammatory and stabilises essential fatty acids against deterioration. Important in brain health, extra-virgin olive oil protects visual functions and improves overall brain function. When cooking with olive oil only heat up to 130°C/266°F. Only buy the extra-virgin varieties and ensure it has been cold-pressed.

FLAXSEED OIL

Although flaxseed contains all sorts of healthy components, it owes its primary healthy reputation to its high Omega-3 essential fatty acids content. Each tablespoon of ground flaxseed contains about 1.8g of plant Omega-3s. It also contains lignans, which have both plant oestrogen and antioxidant qualities. Flax is also high in fibre and contains both the soluble and insoluble types. Flax, also known as linseed, is best used as an oil (which should never be heated) or as the seed. The seed in its complete form cannot be digested by the body and should always be ground before eaten. The high mucilage content of flax also makes it a good binding or drawing agent.

HEMP POWDER/OIL/SEEDS

A seed with an earthy-nutty flavour that is full of Omega-3's, protein, carbohydrates and free of any allergens.

GINGER

Fiery in its flavour, ginger is an incredible immune-boosting plant which helps to fight colds and flu. Anti-inflammatory, antiviral and antibacterial in its properties, it works well for headaches, sleepiness, indigestion, stomach upsets, nausea and motion sickness due to its anti-emetic properties. Also a good hormonal regulator, ginger really is a wonder drug which can be used in its fresh or juiced form or as a powder.

SAGE

Calming sage helps to prime digestion and is the perfect pairing with roasted vegetables such as squash. Antiseptic and antispasmodic in its actions, sage is useful for sore throats, mouth ulcers, and nasal catarrhal conditions. It's my go-to herb for when a gargle is needed to get rid of that sore throat.

ONION
Onions can be used either cooked or raw and act as anti-inflammatory, antibiotic and antiviral agents within the body. Prized as a respiratory antiseptic it helps to break down mucous. A warming expectorant, it also expels the mucous from the body by stimulating circulation. High in sulphur containing amino acids, onions are very good at detoxifying the body from heavy metals.

MOLASSES
Rich in zinc, this thick syrup is actually made from the sugar cane plant to make sugar white. It is rich in flavour and often mixed with other sweeteners so please read the label to ensure you are buying the pure product.

CACAO
Available as a powder, butter, paste, beans and nibs, this is raw, real and unroasted chocolate. Full of antioxidants and magnesium, all cacao products come from a bean. When cracked it produces cacao nibs and when stone-ground produces cacao paste (or liquor). When the fat is extracted and then solidified, cacao butter is produced and what is left is the cacao powder. One of the most antioxidant rich foods known to us, it is also high in magnesium and is the perfect calming stimulant. Don't we all love it!

BEE POLLEN
Although a raw product, bee pollen isn't considered vegan. Prized for its ability to promote endurance and vitality it is used to treat allergies, boost your immune system and slow the ageing process, it is considered one of the worlds most complete foods with an abundance of nutrients.

CHIA SEEDS
A tiny but mighty seed, I am so glad these have been popularised. High in amino acids Omega-3's, fibre, calcium and antioxidants, these little seeds are also a complete protein. In cooking processes these seeds are used to absorb liquid and can be a good egg substitute in baking.

INDEX

ACKNOWLEDGEMENTS

The dream and evolution of this book spans many years and I truly hope I can capture even a small slice of the gratitude I feel towards the people who have helped me fulfil this often all-consuming determination to achieve these pages.

The very first thought of being published came to me when I was living in my little stone cottage in Tuscany in 2009. Those stone walls and the view over the olive trees and vineyard rows filled me with the understanding that life was going to be grande and that anything would be possible as long as I had love and nature all around me.

The decision I made in 2008 to set myself free and explore another aspect of my heritage took me to the other side of the world, far away from my family and loved ones. Leaving and living without them continues to be the hardest thing I do. This book is for them, because they let me flap my wings and travel off to a distant unknown, yet still gave me all the love I needed.

Thanks must also go to: My everything, Tom, you healed me in more ways you could ever have known and continue to inspire and surround me with so much love. A true and genuine soul, I am grateful for your presence in my life everyday.

Nonna, I have felt your presence with me through some of the hardest and most blissful times since you left my side. But you're always there and I could not have done this without you. You are the reason I had this book inside of me and I hope this can be a piece of your legacy on this earth.

Heather Holden-Brown (and inadvertently, Kate Pumphrey) for your guidance and support. Your tireless work is the reason this dream came true.

My editor, Romilly, upon meeting you, I instantly knew you were the person who would help me to publish this book. Your creative energy and vision from that very first meeting instilled a confidence and trust that has helped guide this project along and produce a piece of work I am truly proud to call my own. To Helen, Sarah, Katherine, Nikki and all the other wonderful people at Quadrille, I am truly grateful for all of your hard work.

To the fabulous photographer, Lisa Cohen and food stylist, Deborah Kaloper. I am so very thankful to you for all your creative spirit, inspiration, talent and fun times while bringing this cookbook to life. I could not be more honoured to have had you with me along this journey.

A special thank you must also go to my beautiful Mum who helped me to prepare and cook every recipe for the photo shoot. I am so proud of you and all you have achieved throughout your life and I am so happy you have supported me through mine.

Verity and Simon for choosing to fly me half way across the world and join their gorgeous family. For the gift of your beautiful son, Sam, and the unconditional love he gave me.

Darren Seymour-Russell and Wendy Chant for giving me the opportunity to put my food on show for the very first time and for all the trust and hope they invested in me.

You guys, the book is for **you**! It's so you can go forth and create a connected, healthy temple from which to experience life from. Your body is your greatest asset and gift. Cherish and look after it. If I have managed to help you connect with your body, then I have done my job as a naturopath and educator. I am truly humbled and wish you all good health and happiness along your own journey.

Publishing Director Sarah Lavelle
Creative Director Helen Lewis
Editor Romilly Morgan
Designers Nicola Ellis, Katherine Keeble
Photographer Lisa Cohen
Cover photographer Ali Allen
Food & Prop Stylist Deborah Kaloper
Production Emily Noto, Vincent Smith

First published in 2016 by
Quadrille Publishing
Pentagon House
52–54 Southwark Street
London SE1 1UN
www.quadrille.co.uk
www.quadrille.com

Quadrille is an imprint of Hardie Grant
www.hardiegrant.com.au

Text © 2016 Kimberly Parsons

All photography © 2016 Lisa Cohen with the following
exceptions: Cover photography (author picture) and page 6
© 2016 Ali Allen

Pages 16-17, 44-45, 94-95, 118-119, and back endpaper
Shutterstock; pages 68-69, 142-143 and front endpaper
Getty; pages 166-167 Flowcrete

Cataloguing in Publication Data: a catalogue record for
this book is available from the British Library.

ISBN: 978 184949 899 9

Printed in China

*The publisher wishes to thank Magic Carpets Yoga Mats
http://magiccarpetym.com for the loan of the yoga mats
on page 6.*